KNOWLEDGE-BASED RISK MANAGEMENT IN ENGINEERING

KNOWLEDGE-BASED RISK MANAGEMENT IN ENGINEERING: A CASE STUDY IN HUMAN–COMPUTER COOPERATIVE SYSTEMS

KIYOSHI NIWA

Senior Researcher—Advanced Research Laboratory,
Hitachi, Ltd., Tokyo
   and Senior Research Fellow—
IC^2 Institute
The University of Texas at Austin

WILEY

A WILEY-INTERSCIENCE PUBLICATION
JOHN WILEY & SONS
NEW YORK   CHICHESTER   BRISBANE   TORONTO   SINGAPORE

Library of Congress Cataloging-in-Publication Data:

Niwa, Kiyoshi.
  Knowledge-based risk management in engineering.

  (Wiley series in engineering and technology management)
  "A Wiley-Interscience publication."
  Includes bibliographies and index.
  1. Engineering—Management—Data processing. 2. Expert
systems (Computer science) 3. Technology—Risk assess-
ment. I. Title. II. Series.
TA190.N58 1988   658   88–33833
ISBN 0–471–62893–X

Printed in the United States of America

10 9 8 7 6 5 4 3 2 1

CONTENTS

PREFACE

This book addresses the application of artificial intelligence (AI) to management, an attempt to attain a new level of AI, and risk management for large construction projects. Its purpose is to present a new concept, a "human–computer cooperative system," as the next-generation knowledge-based system for application to ill-structured management fields.

We are advancing rapidly into a postindustrial, information-intensive society. Through worldwide networks and a number of large databases, almost all necessary data can easily be obtained except knowledge that domain specialists have obtained through experience. Therefore, such knowledge will increase its relative value in many fields, especially in engineering, management, and business. Recently, AI or its subspecialty, expert systems (also called knowledge-based systems), has attracted special interest in order to deal with such domain specialists' knowledge.

This book is based on my 10 years of research, development, and implementation of knowledge-based systems for project risk management. In this book, first a common expert system will be developed. Then its weak points in terms of being applied to ill-structured management domains will be identified based on users' complaints about the system. Finally, a human–computer cooperative system will be proposed to overcome these weak points. The main purpose of the human–computer cooperative system is to explicitly incorporate human intuitive ability into the computer system. A case study is used involving a risk management case for large construction projects; however, discussions and methods described in this book can be applied to other management fields.

In fact, this book can be used for a wide range of purposes:

- *Graduate courses in engineering and business* can use it as a textbook for application of AI to engineering/project management. Currently, there are few books available for this purpose, although this necessity has recently been stressed.

- *Graduate courses in expert systems* can use it as required reading, since it demonstrates limitations of current expert systems as well as approaches to overcome these limitations.

- *AI and anti-AI professionals* can use this book as a source of ideas for their research activities because it explores a new AI frontier (i.e., explicitly using human intuitive ability).

- *Knowledge engineers* who experience difficulties in applying AI systems to management fields can use this as a reference book, since they can find recommended procedures to handle ill-structured management fields, as well as useful lessons for developing the systems.

- *Risk managers, engineering managers, project managers, and construction managers* can use it as a guidebook for their activities because the central subject in the case study is how to transfer risk experience within organizations. This has been a crucial area to be developed in such management fields.

KIYOSHI NIWA

Tokyo, Japan
November, 1988

ACKNOWLEDGMENTS

The support of Hitachi, Ltd., in the research and writing of this book is greatly appreciated. Dr. Takeo Miura gave me the opportunity to conduct this research. Messrs. Yasuhiro Yamaji, Isao Fujine, Yukio Watanabe, and Kazutoshi Meguro played important roles in applying the system to actual projects. Ms. Yumiko Iizuka assisted me with the computer programming. Dr. Eiichi Maruyama gave me the opportunity to write this book.

Special thanks are due Dr. Yutaka Saeki of Tokyo University for his stimulating discussions on the cognitive psychology aspects of this research. I also would like to thank Dr. George Kozmetsky of the University of Texas at Austin, Dr. Andrew P. Sage of George Mason University, and Dr. Edward A. Feigenbaum of Stanford University for their helpful discussions on this research.

I also express my appreciation to Mr. Munehisa Sakuyama of Chiyoda Corporation for his valuable comments on project management and risk management.

This book is partly based on my thesis for my doctor of engineering degree. I express my deepest appreciation to Dr. Takehiko Matsuda of SANNO College, Dr. Shigenobu Kobayashi, and Dr. Bunpei Nakano of the Tokyo Institute of Technology for their continuing guidance and encouragement in completing this thesis.

I also thank Dr. Dundar E. Kocaoglu, Series Editor of the Wiley Series in Engineering and Technology Management, as well as Mr. Frank J. Cerra, Editor, for their kind comments.

___1
INTRODUCTION

This chapter presents the scope and objectives of this book as well as explaining why and how our new concept, a "human–computer cooperative system," was developed. Next, an outline of the chapters is provided in order to help readers to grasp the organization of the book and understand the discussions in each chapter. Finally, some related fields are described that involve AI/expert systems, human–computer interaction, project management, business/project risk management, civil engineering, management science and operations research, and decision support systems. Original and different ideas that relate to these fields are briefly described.

1.1 SCOPE AND OBJECTIVES

The purpose of this book is to present a new concept, *human–computer cooperative system,* in applying artificial intelligence (AI) to ill-structured management domains. This concept will be a key to successful computer applications in the coming "information-intensive" society, in which many kinds of ill-structured knowledge will play important roles. This concept was not produced by theoretical thinking alone. It was based on 10 years of actual system practice (Niwa et al., 1979, 1981a, 1981b, 1982, 1983, 1984, 1986, 1988a, 1988b), which has included a persistent search for a useful

1

system, careful deliberation of human–computer relationships, and effective employment of multidisciplinary approaches consisting of AI, management science, and systems thinking.

Therefore, to understand this new concept, it is helpful for readers to go through an experience similar to this. This is why the book is organized as a case study.

A "large-project risk management" case is used in this book. This has been a very critical problem in actual project/engineering management fields. Therefore, those who are primarily interested in project/engineering management (and who have not so far been interested in AI) will also find this book very useful because we will present a computer system for project risk management that has not yet been studied in depth. In addition, these readers will find themselves becoming familiar with fundamentals of AI and its new frontier (i.e., human–computer cooperative systems) which we will develop.

The case study problem in this book was originally described as follows (Niwa et al., 1979):

> Dramatic changes in the world economic balance in the early 1970s have spawned many large construction projects in developing countries, especially in the Middle East. In the process of carrying out these projects, a great number of "risks," defined here as undesirable events such as troubles and accidents which cause project delays or excess expenditures, have been known to occur. This has been primarily due to the dramatic escalation in the size and scope of projects, and contractor's lack of experience in these countries. Consequently, development of methods or tools to assist project managers in achieving more effective control over these risks has become an urgent task.

The computerized system described in this book is basically a form of a knowledge-based system. This system is designed to assist project managers in achieving more effective control over risks by providing them with appropriate knowledge, gathered from many project managers and compiled into a knowledge base. It is designed to warn project managers of risks that may follow from causes they have specified, as well as to confirm or deny hypothetical risks based on a model of risk causes.

From a methodological point of view, the most interesting aspect should be how to create the new concept of a human–computer cooperative system in applying AI to the preceding case study. After analyzing the character of project risks, one finds that "knowledge transfer" among project managers is critical to project risk management. Consequently, an expert system should be developed for that purpose. This by itself is ambitious because there have been few expert systems in management domains that consist of ill-structured knowledge.

Unexpected problems appear when we seem to complete the system development in that managers do not want to continue using the system. They claim that the system is not an "expert system" but a "novice system." More precisely, it is not a system "for experts or managers" but "for novices." In actual business fields, there are very few novice managers whereas most are average managers (and very few are excellent managers). To solve real-world problems, therefore, a system must be developed for average project managers.

Attention should be paid to the fact that average project managers employ not only logical thinking (similar to expert system inference), but also "intuitive thinking" (not logical thinking) in everyday management processes. Upon hearing about "intuitive thinking," many computer researchers and developers do not like to continue in such a vague field. In addition, some "anti-AI" people criticize the lack of intuitive thinking in current expert systems (e.g., Dreyfus and Dreyfus, 1986). However, dealing with intuitive thinking seems to be an unavoidable task if development of a knowledge-based system for management domains is possible. In this way, a new approach that incorporates human intuitive processes into a system as one of its subsystems will be proposed.

1.2   OVERVIEW

This book is composed of nine chapters. Chapter 1 outlines the scope and objectives of the book. In Chapter 2, risks are defined as problems and accidents that cause project delays, cost overruns, or deficiencies in technical performance. Engineering firm surveys found that many similar risks recur in the execution stage of large construction projects. A knowledge transfer system is proposed to reduce the recurrence of risks. The four system functions are determined through an analysis of project managers' requirements, as well as the characteristics of risk management in large construction projects. The four functions are

1. Collecting a large amount of experience,
2. Adapting to many projects,
3. Analyzing risk-causing mechanisms, and
4. Improving abilities.

Chapter 3 outlines expert systems and presents the relationships between expert systems and human–computer cooperative systems. First, expert system characteristics are identified as

1. Use of a knowledge base that consists of domain specialists' knowledge,
2. Use of an inference mechanism, and
3. An attempt to solve real-world problems.

Next, some current issues and limitations of expert systems are discussed in terms of these three characteristics. Some approaches to overcoming these limitations are presented. Finally, future directions of expert system research are presented. These include analytic strategy, improvement strategy, and goal-oriented strategy. The human–computer cooperative system corresponds to the last strategy.

Methods and procedures of knowledge acquisition as well as the knowledge that is obtained is discussed in Chapter 4. First, to determine the scope of the knowledge that should be acquired, the domain knowledge is analyzed so that a "risk mechanism model" and a "standard work package method" are developed. Then, procedures for acquiring such knowledge are discussed based on our actual experience. Finally, many hundreds of risks that actually happened, or nearly happened, during many projects have been demonstrated.

Chapter 5 discusses knowledge representations of the knowledge base for project risk management. Four typical knowledge representation schemes (semantic network, production system, structured production system, and frame) are briefly overviewed and categorized according to two dimensions (i.e., in terms of their declarative/procedural and uniform/structured characteristics). The character of risk management knowledge is then discussed from the same viewpoint. In this way, the structured production system is shown to be the suitable knowledge representation because the characteristics of both the structured production system and risk management knowledge are procedural and structured. In addition, experimental and quantitative comparisons of these knowledge representation schemes are performed. This also shows the advantages of the structured production system, namely, its ease in implementing the knowledge base and inference engine, as well as its run time efficiency.

Knowledge utilization methods of the knowledge base for project risk management is discussed in Chapter 6. Forward and backward reasoning, which are common AI techniques, are first discussed. Forward reasoning is found effective for project managers in forecasting risks that would occur because of the causes that they input. Backward reasoning is found effective in checking the occurrence probability of hypothesized risks. However, as project managers become accustomed to these inference methods, they will no longer be satisfied with them. This is because project managers will feel that the answers provided by a system using such methods are too limited, since they know that there may be other knowledge that should be available in the knowledge base for solving their problems. Therefore, a new frontier of expert systems to overcome such user complaints will be investigated.

The objective of Chapter 7 is to present a new concept, a "human–computer cooperative system," and to integrate the discussions of the previous chapters. In an exploration of the future roles of computers, the new concept is presented. Then, a human–computer cooperative system for project risk management is developed. System functions are designed according to the requirement analysis presented in Chapter 2. Knowledge, obtained as described in Chapter 4, is stored in the kowledge base with a structured production system representation scheme as determined in Chapter 5. Knowledge utilization is applied by the methods described in Chapter 6. These are forward and backward reasoning as well as knowledge association methods. Next, this chapter demonstrates examples of the system in use. Finally, after describing users' positive and negative evaluations of the system, some potential application fields of the system are presented.

Chapter 8 presents 19 lessons for successful implementation of knowledge-based systems. These lessons have been obtained during 10 years of R&D and implementation of knowledge-based systems, including ordinary expert systems and human–computer cooperative systems. These lessons are described in the three phases of system planning, system development, and system maintenance.

Chapter 9 offers concluding remarks in terms of three aspects: human–computer cooperative systems, project risk management, and future research.

1.3   RELATED FIELDS

1.3.1   AI and Expert Systems

AI, in its general sense, is the main subject of this book. However, compared with "proper" AI (e.g., Barr and Feigenbaum, 1981, 1982; Cohen and Feigenbaum, 1982) and expert systems (e.g., Hayes-Roth et al, 1983; Waterman, 1986), this book presents a new category of AI application (i.e., to ill-structured management domains). This is why this book can bring readers to one of the new frontiers of AI, which uses human intuitive ability.

Chapter 3 overviews AI and expert systems and discusses some of their fundamental issues and limitations, as well as approaches to overcoming these limitations and some possible future research strategies. These discussions will clarify the differences and relationships between current expert systems and our new approach, the human–computer cooperative system.

1.3.2 Human–Computer Interaction

The main idea of this book, "human–computer cooperative systems," reminds one of "human–computer interaction," which is a vital area of recent computer interface research (e.g., Badre and Shneiderman, 1982; Card et al., 1983; Norman and Draper, 1986; Vassiliou, 1984; Woods, 1985). The main idea of the human–computer interaction is to design computer interfaces to match human cognitive processes. More specifically, the chief objective is to make computer systems easy to learn and use (Sondheimer and Relles, 1982). In addition, the essential reason for our proposing a human–computer cooperative system in this book is that, in ill-structured management domains, it is indispensable for better management to effectively combine human intuitive ability with the logical functions of a computer in a cooperative system.

1.3.3 Project Management

It has been pointed out that integrated use of vast amounts of knowledge obtained through experience is important for better project management (e.g., Souder, 1979; Stuckenbruck, 1977). Knowledge-based systems can extend the range and power of conventional computer systems for project management, as a recent study (Levitt and Kunz, 1987) indicated. However, until now, most knowledge-based techniques have been applied to schedule planning and control (e.g., Levitt and Kunz, 1985; Sathi et al., 1986), whereas very few techniques (Niwa and Sasaki, 1983) have been applied to project management in which effective use of many kinds of knowledge is critical. This is largely because of the fact that today's project control computer systems are mostly based on network techniques, in which the main functions are project planning, project performance measurement, and cost-schedule integration within a project Work Breakdown Structure (WBS) (Project Management Institute, 1981; Cleland and King, 1983). Therefore, the case study in this book is one of the earliest developments of a knowledge-based project management system.

1.3.4   Business/Project Risk Management

Since the cost of risk in business today is growing for many corporations, it is essential to create a risk management function within the corporate structure, including risk managers with sufficient background in all related fields (Boodman, 1987). This book presents the framework of a system to assist in providing such risk managers with necessary knowledge of related fields.

Various papers have been published particularly in the project risk management field. At the project feasibility study (or preproposal preparation) stage, risk analysis for investment (e.g., Cozzolino, 1979; Hall, 1975; Hertz, 1964, 1968) and forecasts of country risk (e.g., Bunn and Mustafaoglu, 1978; Haner, 1979; Rummel and Heenan, 1978; Stobaugh, 1969) have been the main research areas. At the project planning or proposal preparation stage, many papers have appeared on the estimation of probability of cost overruns or project delays, and the amount of contingency (e.g., Anderson, 1969; Carrier, 1978; Chapman, 1979; Traylor et al, 1978) and its effect on competitive bidding (e.g., Bjornsson, 1979; Pentico, 1985). At the project execution stage, the primary effort should be focused on identifying risks and preventing them in advance, which seems suitable to knowledge-based systems, although little research has yet been reported. This book focuses on the project execution stage.

1.3.5   Other Fields

This book proposes a new concept/system, a human-computer cooperative system, as the next-generation knowledge-based system, which can be applied to the following fields in which effective use of AI and knowledge-based systems has recently been stressed to improve problem-solving capabilities:

- Knowledge-based systems offer new and potentially valuable capabilities to support decision making in *civil engineering,* with the goal of reducing costs (Kim et al., 1986).

- To successfully solve real-world management problems, *management science (MS) and operations research (OR)* must use the AI tools that can be applied to ill-structured, knowledge-rich, nonquantitative decision domains (Simon, 1987).
- *Decision support systems (DSS),* proposed in the late 1970s and early 1980s (Keen and Morton, 1978), have progressed to incorporate AI and expert systems (e.g., Dhar and Croker, 1988; Fordyce et al., 1986; Luconi et al., 1986; Methlie and Sprague, 1985; Sage and Lagomasino, 1982, 1987).

REFERENCES

Anderson, R. M., "Handling risk in defense contracting," *Harvard Business Review,* July–August, p. 90, 1969.

Badre, A., and B. Shneiderman (eds.), *Directions in Human/Computer Interaction,* Ablex, Norwood, NJ, 1982.

Barr, A., and E. A. Feigenbaum, *The Handbook of Artificial Intelligence,* Vol. 1, William Kaufmann, Los Altos, CA, 1981.

Barr, A., and E. A. Feigenbaum, *The Handbook of Artificial Intelligence,* Vol. 2, William Kaufmann, Los Altos, CA, 1982.

Bjornsson, H., "Cost uncertainties and bidding," *Technical Paper of Department of Civil Engineering,* University of Illinois at Urbana–Champaign, 1979.

Boodman, D. M., "Managing business risk," *Interfaces,* **17**(2), p. 91, 1987.

Bunn, D. W., and M. M. Mustafaoglu, "Forecasting political risk," *Management Science,* **24,** p. 1557, November 1978.

Card, S. K., T. P. Moran, and A. Newell, *The Psychology of Human–Computer Interaction,* Lawrence Erlbaum Associates, Hillsdale, NJ, 1983.

Carrier, K. C., "Contingency," *Project Management Quarterly,* **9**(4), p. 25, 1978.

Chapman, C. B., "Large engineering project risk analysis," *IEEE Transactions on Engineering Management,* **EM-26**(3), p. 78, 1979.

Cleland, D. I., and W. R. King, (eds.), *Project Management Handbook,* Van Nostrand Reinhold, New York, 1983.

Cohen, P. R., and E. A. Feigenbaum, *The Handbook of Artificial Intelligence,* Vol. 3, William Kaufmann, Los Altos, CA, 1982.

Cozzolino, J. M., "A new method for risk analysis," *Sloan Management Review,* p. 53, Spring, 1979.

Dhar, V., and A. Croker, "Knowledge based decision support in business: Issues and a solution," *IEEE Expert,* **3,** p. 53, 1988.

Dreyfus, H. L., and S. E. Dreyfus, *Mind Over Machine—The Power of Human Intuition and Expertise in the Era of the Computer,* Free Press, New York, 1986.

Fordyce, K., P. Norden, and G. Sullivan, "Artificial intelligence and the management science practitioner: Expert systems—Getting a handle on a moving target," *Interfaces,* **16**(6), p. 61, 1986.

Hall, W. K., "Why risk analysis isn't working," *Long Range Planning,* p. 25, December 1975.

Haner, F. T., "Rating investment risks abroad," *Business Horizon,* p. 18, April 1979.

Hayes-Roth, F., D. A. Waterman, and D. B. Lenat (eds.), *Bulling Expert Systems,* Addison-Wesley, Reading, MA, 1983.

Hertz, D. B., "Risk analysis in capital investment," *Harvard Business Review,* January–February, p. 95, 1964.

Hertz, D. B., "Investment policies that pay off," *Harvard Business Review,* January–February, p. 96, 1968.

Keen, P. G. W., and M. S. Scott Morton, *Decision Support Systems: An Organization Perspective,* Addison-Wesley, Reading, MA, 1978.

Kim, S. S., M. L. Maher, R. E. Levitt, M. F. Rooney, T. J. Siller, and S. G. Richie, "Survey of the state-of-the-art expert/knowledge based systems in civil engineering," *USA-CERL Special Report,* P-87/01, 1986.

Levitt, R. E., and J. C. Kunz, "Using knowledge of construction and project management for automated schedule updating," *Project Management Journal,* **16**(5), p. 57, 1985.

Levitt, R. E., and J. C. Kunz, "Using artificial intelligence techniques to support project management," *Artificial Intelligence for Engineering Design, Analysis and Manufacturing* (AI EDAM), **1**(1), p. 3, 1987.

Luconi, F. L., T. W. Malone, and M. S. Scott Morton, "Expert Systems: The next challenge for managers," *Sloan Management Review,* **27**(4), p. 3, 1986.

Methlie, L. B., and R. H. Sprague, Jr. (eds.), *Knowledge Representation for Decision Support Systems,* North-Holland, Amsterdam, 1985.

Niwa, K., M. Okuma, S. Seki, and I. Fujine, "Development of a risk alarm system for big construction projects," *Proc. of Project Management Institute Symposium,* p. 221, 1979.

Niwa, K., "Definition of risks," in *The Japan Society of Industrial Machinery Manufacturers, A Joint Study for Foreign Project Risk Management,* p. 25, 1981a.

Niwa, K., "Trouble library," in *The Japan Society of Industrial Machinery Manufacturers, A Joint Study for Foreign Project Risk Management,* p. 114, 1981b.

Niwa, K., and M. Okuma, "Know-how transfer method and its application to risk management for large construction projects," *IEEE Transactions on Engineering Management,* **EM-29**(4), p. 146, 1982.

Niwa, K., and K. Sasaki, "A new project management system approach: The know-how based project management system," *Project Management Quarterly,* **14**(1), p. 65, 1983.

Niwa, K., K. Sasaki, and H. Ihara, "An experimental comparison of knowledge representation schemes," *AI Magazine,* **5**(2), p. 29, 1984.

Niwa, K., "Knowledge-based human–computer cooperative system for ill-structured management domains," *IEEE Transactions on Systems, Man, and Cybernetics,* **SMC-16**(3), p. 335, 1986.

Niwa, K., "Knowledge transfer: A key to successful application of knowledge-based systems," *The Knowledge Engineering Review,* **2**(3), Special Issue on Technology Transfer, p. 145, 1988a.

Niwa, K., "Human–computer cooperative system: Conceptual basis, sample system evaluation, and R&D directions," *Proc. of American Society of Mechanical Engineers Manufacturing International,* p. 87, 1988b.

Norman, D. A., and S. W. Draper (eds.), *User Centered System Design: New Perspectives on Human–Computer Interaction,* Lawrence Erlbaum Associates, Hillsdale, NJ, 1986.

Pentico, D. W., "Estimating project costs with regression and risk analysis," *Project Management Journal,* **16**(1), p. 58, 1985.

Project Management Institute, *The Implementation of Project Management: The Professional's Handbook,* Addison-Wesley, Reading, MA, 1981.

Rummel, R. J., and D. A. Heenan, "How multinationals analyze political risk," *Harvard Business Review,* January–February, p. 67, 1978.

Sage, A. P., and A. Lagomasino, "Knowledge representation and interpretation in decision support systems," *Proc. of IEEE International Conference of Cybernetics and Society,* p. 658, 1982.

Sage, A. P., and A. Lagomasino, "Computer-based intelligent support: An integrated expert systems and decision support systems approach," In B. G. Silverman (ed.), *Expert Systems for Business,* Addison-Wesley, Reading, MA, 1987.

Sathi, A., T. E. Morton, and S. F. Roth, "Callisto: An intelligent project management system," *AI Magazine,* **7**(5), p. 34, 1986.

Simon, H. A., "Two heads are better than one: The collaboration between AI and OR," *Interfaces,* **17**(4), p. 8, 1987.

Sondheimer, N. K., and N. Relles, "Human factors and user assistance in interactive computing systems: An introduction," *IEEE Transactions on Systems, Man, and Cybernetics,* **SMC-12**(2), p. 102, 1982.

Souder, W. E., "Project management: Past, present, and future—An editorial summary," *IEEE Transactions on Engineering Management,* **EM-26**(3), p. 49, 1979.

Stobaugh, R. B., "How to analyze foreign investment climates," *Harvard Business Review,* September–October, p. 100, 1969.

Stuckenbruck, L. C., "The educational path to project management," *Proc. of Project Management Institute Symposium,* p. 425, 1977.

Traylor, R. C., R. C. Stinson, J. L. Madsen, R. S. Bell, and K. R. Brown, "Project management under uncertainty," *Proc. of Project Management Institute Symposium,* p. II-F., 1, 1978.

Vassiliou, Y. (ed.), *Human Factors and Interactive Computer Systems,* Ablex, Norwood, NJ, 1984.

Waterman, D. A., *A Guide to Expert Systems,* Addison-Wesley, Reading, MA, 1986.

Woods, D. D., "Cognitive technologies: The design of joint human–machine cognitive systems," *AI Magazine,* **6**(4), p. 86, 1985.

____2
REQUIREMENTS
FOR MANAGING
PROJECT RISKS

The objective of this chapter is to determine the functions required of project risk management systems. First of all, the term *risk* is defined because there is no suitable definition available for our purposes. Next, through analyzing actual risks and surveying large engineering companies, key risk characteristics are identified on which our system development efforts are focused. Finally, the system functions are determined based on project managers' requirements and system purposes. These functions are the basis of the system that will be developed in the following chapters.

2.1 DEFINITION OF PROJECT RISKS

2.1.1 Definition of Project Risks in This Book

According to a survey (Niwa, 1981a) in 1981, most engineering enterprises in America, Europe, and Japan at that time did not have definitions of project risk. However, it had become very common for people in engineering or project management circles to say "It's risky" when certain problems arose in engineering or construction projects.* These problems had been

*The author made a presentation at the Project Management Institute (PMI) 1979 Symposium in Atlanta, GA, entitled "Development of a Risk Alarm System for Big Construction Projects." The Japan Society of Industrial Machinery Manufacturers organized the Foreign Project Risk Management Committee in 1980.

known to occur in various stages of construction projects such as shown in Fig. 2.1. Some of these problems involve:

- Problems in the contractual stage:
    Differences in the interpretation of provisions when the other party changes the person in charge of the contract.
- Problems in the design stage:
    Design errors due to lack of accurate data.
    Delay in owner approval of design plans.
- Problems in the procurement stage:
    Equipment reorders due to oversights of foreign standards.
    Bankruptcy of local manufacturers.
- Problems in the transportation stage:
    Additional payment to inland transportation companies due to late ship arrivals.
    Transport delays due to infrastructure deficiencies (roads, bridges, harbors, etc.).
- Problems in the supervisor dispatch stage:

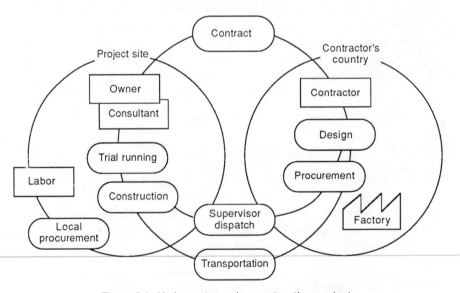

Figure 2.1. Various stages in construction project.

Additional cost for returning to a home country because of unavailability of working visa.

- Problems in the construction stage:

    Delay in welding work due to labor strikes.

    Frustrations among engineers due to communication gaps with local workers.

- Problems in the trial-running stage:

    Interruption of trial running due to political unrest.

    Unexpected test items due to owner's requests.

Because there are many types of risk, there is sometimes confusion when discussing risk with project managers, project personnel, or top management. Therefore, we have defined project risks in this book as "undesirable events, such as problems and accidents, which cause project delays, cost overruns, or deficiencies in technical performance." The first version of this definition was presented in 1979 (Niwa et al., 1979) after a three-year study analyzed hundreds of actual cases. Risk definition has been given from the viewpoint of our intended purpose of dealing with actual problems, such as those mentioned above, and minimizing their adverse effects.

More detailed discussions about project risks, such as causes of risks or risk occurrence mechanisms, will be presented in Section 4.1 "Analysis of Domain Knowledge" and Section 4.3, "Obtained Knowledge." Subsequent part of this section provides a brief survey of other risk definitions in related fields.

2.1.2 Risk Definitions in Related Fields

Insurance Field. In the insurance field, it has been said that there is no "correct" definition of risk. Instead textbook writers have defined risk in various ways (Williams and Heins, 1976). For example, (Vaughan, 1986)

If we were to survey the best-known insurance textbooks used in colleges and universities today, we would find a general lack of agreement concerning the definition of risk. In general, we would find the term defined in one of the following ways:

1. Risk is the chance of loss.
2. Risk is the possibility of loss.
3. Risk is uncertainty.

4. Risk is the dispersion of actual from expected results.

5. Risk is the probability of any outcome different from the one expected.

Definitions 1 and 2 seem applicable to the many kinds of project risks mentioned above when the phrase "chance of" or "possibility of" (i.e., the concept of "prior to the fact") is appended to them. However, this idea does not fit our purpose because, for example, after a risk occurs, countermeasures are possible and sometimes very important in project risk management fields. Definition 3 is too vague for us to use. The use of definitions 4 and 5 depends on whether these project risks were foreseen. This is a rather subjective issue that could cause difficulties, for example, in selecting suitable risks from among a collection of risk experiences of many project managers. Thus, it has been difficult for us to use insurance risk definitions.

Decision Theory. In the field of operations research or management science, and, more specifically, in decision theory (e.g., Chernoff and Moses, 1959; Fishburn, 1964; Savage, 1954), the traditional definition of risk proceeds as follows (Arnoff and Sengupta, 1961). Decisions in stochastic problems are based on probability distributions of relevant parameters (e.g., unit costs, selling prices, demand, and so on). Of concern are cases where such parameters are not unique. Situations are distinguished by two broad types (Hart, 1941; Tintner, 1941):

1. Those in which the parameters have known probability distribution functions—*risky* situations, and

2. Those in which the nature of the distribution function is not known—*uncertain* situations.

The definition of risk in decision theory, therefore, is too strict to apply to our problems.

Project Management Field. Recently, in the project management field, it was proposed that risk management be added to the project management body of knowledge as a separately identifiable management function (Wideman, 1986):

In the context of project management, project risk may be defined as the chance of certain occurrences adversely affecting project objectives (Cleland, 1985; Wideman, 1983). It is the degree of exposure to negative events, and their probable consequences. Project risk is therefore characterized by the following risk factors:

1. The risk event (i.e., precisely what might happen to the detriment of the project),
2. The risk probability (i.e., how likely the event is to occur), and
3. The amount at stake (i.e., the extent of loss which could result).

Therefore, our "risk" term coincides with the above "risk event" term. The preceding "risk factor" is different from our risk factor that is introduced in Chapter 4 in terms of the causes of risk. We develop a risk occurrence mechanism model in Section 4.1 using our risk and risk factor terms.

2.2   RECURRENCE OF SIMILAR RISKS

According to the definition of project risks, actual cases have been collected of risks that happened during large construction projects such as thermal power stations, gas-turbine power stations, and substation plants. Attention has been focused on turnkey projects in foreign countries because many risks have been known to occur in such projects. Certainly every individual project manager has experienced a strange or new risk that could not have been foreseen. However, it was sometimes found that another project manager in the same department had already encountered the same, or at least a very similar, risk in a different project. When considered this from the viewpoint of the entire company, it was discovered that many similar risks recurred.

In order to confirm that similar risks recur in large engineering/construction projects, we investigated risk similarity in large engineering companies in America and Europe. This investigation was made as one of the survey items conducted by the Foreign Project Risk Management Committee, involving the author as a member, and was organized by the Japan Society of Industrial Machinery Manufacturers in 1981. The results of the investigation of eight European and American engineering companies (Niwa, 1981b) are shown in Fig. 2.2. For three of the eight companies (a, b, and c), most (80–100%) of the risks are the same as those experienced previously by those companies. For the next four companies (d, e, f, and g), many (50–79%) of the risks are the same as those experienced previously by those companies. The remaining company replied that some (0–49%) risks recurred. These results were obtained by interviewing top executives (e.g.,

Similarity / Company	Most 80-100 %	Many 50—79 %	Some 0—49%
a	x		
b	x		
c	x		
d		x	
e		x	
f		x	
g		x	
h			x

Figure 2.2. Similarity of risks. (From Niwa, 1981b. Reprinted with permission of The Japan Society of Industrial Machinery Manufacturers.)

vice presidents) or heads of project management/engineering departments. Therefore, from the corporate viewpoint, it is reasonable to assume that similar risks recur in large construction projects.

The following items may be causes of recurrence of similar risks in large construction projects:

- Unlike R&D projects, construction projects have a high degree of repetition. That is, work is often done that is similar to work done before. Consequently, the same types of risk are likely to occur.
- As projects become larger and more long term, the number of projects experienced by each project manager during his career decreases. As a result, the domain knowledge that an individual project manager has gained from his own experience becomes insufficient for the large task at hand.
- It is generally difficult to transfer experience or knowledge gained on a previous project.

The relationships of these items are diagrammed in Fig. 2.3.

This book concentrates on preventing recurrence of similar risks in project risk management. Preventing risk recurrence certainly contributes to im-

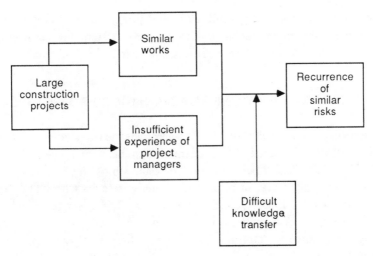

Figure 2.3. Causes of recurrence of similar risks in large construction projects.

proving company profits since most risks are known to recur as described above. Although managing completely new risks is an important and ambitious task, that task is excluded from the scope of this book.

Various strategies can be used to prevent risk recurrence. Some of these strategies involve:

- Give works only to experienced project managers,
- Educate excellent project managers, and
- Develop knowledge transfer systems.

Giving works only to experienced or excellent project managers has an immediate effect. This strategy may be similar to what has been called "relocation" of people as an effective means of technology transfer (Bieber, 1969; Moore, 1969; Rothwell 1978; Stewart, 1969). The problem remains, however, if there are not enough experienced project managers available. Therefore, in addition to this, another strategy may be to educate and train excellent project managers. Recently, an attempt was made to add "risk management" to the project management body of knowledge as a separately identifiable management function (Wideman, 1986). Some of the necessary abilities may be provided by universities in the near future, although it must be admitted that educating good project managers who can succeed in actual business circumstances is an extremely difficult task. Consequently, the third strategy, dealt with here, should be to develop a knowledge transfer system so that the risk experiences of some project managers may be available to many other project managers.

2.3 REQUIRED FUNCTIONS FOR MANAGING PROJECT RISKS

This section establishes the functions of a knowledge transfer system (which we will call the "project risk management system") for preventing recurrence of project risks. The procedure for establishing the functions of the system, often called system requirement analysis (e.g., Checkland, 1981; Miser and Quade, 1985; Quade and Boucher, 1968), is one of the most important processes of system development activities because established functions will directly determine the user interface or input/output of the system.

As a first step in the system requirement analysis, a number of interviews and meetings were held with many project managers to determine their requirements for a project risk management system (Niwa et al., 1979). These requirements have been integrated into the following four items:

(a) Managers want to be informed of the risks that actually happened during similar projects in the past.
(b) Managers want to be able to recognize risks that correspond to the size of the work element* they want.
(c) Managers want risk alarms in advance.
(d) Managers want to be informed of risks from many aspects that cannot be predicted in advance, if possible.

The second step of system requirement analysis is to review the purpose of the system (i.e., to prevent recurrence of project risks) from the broadest possible perspective. The following four features that should be considered have been identified:

1. Large (project),
2. Construction project (management),
3. Risk management, and
4. Computer system.

*The definition of work element (word package) is presented in Section 4.1.

These have been selected because the subject being developed is a risk management computer system for large construction projects.

The third step is the main part of the system requirement analysis. We will describe it in some detail by using Fig. 2.4. The preceeding four features are placed in the left column of Fig. 2.4. The managers' four requirements, from (a) to (d), are placed in the right column of Fig. 2.4.

The first feature is "large," which is located in the top of the left column. This means that there is a great variety and volume of knowledge beyond an individual project manager's experience or ability to digest. Consequently, the system is expected to be able to collect a large amount of experience and knowledge—this is the first required system function described in the top center column. This function should be developed so as to satisfy project managers' requirements of being informed of risks that were actually manifested during similar projects in the past. This requirement is located in the top right column.

"Construction project," located in the left column, differs from the others. However, from the viewpoint of system usefulness, it is necessary to develop a system that is adaptable to many construction projects—this is the second required system function. This function should be developed in order to satisfy project managers' requirement of being able to recognize risks that correspond to the size of the work element they want.

The third feature, "risk management," analyzes risk causes. This is a key to effective risk management because it enables project managers to be warned of risks in advance.

The last feature is the "computer system," which should be capable of informing managers of risks from many aspects that cannot be predicted

Features of the Subject	Functions Required of the System	Project Manager's Requirements
1. Large (Project)	To collect a large amount of experience.	(a) Managers want to be informed of the risks that actually happened during similar projects in the past.
2. Construction Project (Management)	To be adaptable to many construction projects.	(b) Managers want to be able to recognize risks that correspond to the size of the work element they want.
3. Risk Management	To analyze cause and risk mechanisms.	(c) Managers want risk alarms in advance.
4. Computer System	Improved abilities.	(d) Managers want to be informed of risks from many aspects that cannot be predicted in advance, if possible.

Figure 2.4. System requirements.

in advance, which is project managers' requirement (d). (This requirement cannot be satisfied by common expert system techniques. It will be discussed in detail in Section 6.2)

The subsequent chapters from 4 to 7 will discuss and develop the above four functions and integrate them into our newly proposed human–computer cooperative system. The rest of this section outlines system development policies that will be applied in the subsequent chapters.

In collecting large amounts of experience, a goal is to integrate expertise from many project managers. This will be systematically stored in the computer system to function as a knowledge base that effectively offers "risk alarms" to project managers. In order to accomplish the second function of adapting the system to many construction projects, particular attention will be paid to the common characteristics of construction projects. A "work package" concept, defined by pairing the project activity and the equipment/building, will then be devised. This enables risks to be connected to many projects, as is shown in Chapter 4. In regard to the analysis of cause and risk mechanisms for providing risk alarms in advance, a risk mechanism model is developed in Chapter 4. This is then represented by production rules in Chapter 5. To achieve the fourth function, a new method that can retrieve nonlogically related knowledge from the knowledge base is proposed in Chapter 6. These elements are integrated into a human–computer cooperative system in Chapter 7.

2.4 SUMMARY

This chapter defined project risks as "undesirable events, such as problems and accidents, which cause project delays, cost overruns, or deficiencies in technical performance." Relationships between this definition and other definitions in related fields, such as insurance, decision theory, and project management, were briefly overviewed. Through an analysis of risks that actually occurred as well as a survey of engineering companies, we focused our attention on preventing the recurrence of similar risks for better project risk management.

A knowledge transfer system was proposed for this purpose, which is called the project risk management system. The system's four functions are to collect a large amount of experience (i.e., domain specialists' knowledge), to be adaptable to many projects, to analyze risk causes and mechanisms, and to have improved abilities. Our fundamental policies for achieving these functions were described briefly.

REFERENCES

Arnoff, E. L., and S. S. Sengupta, "Mathematical programming," In R. L. Ackoff (ed.), *Progress in Operations Research,* Vol. 1., Operations Research Society of America, Publications in Operations Research No. 5, John Wiley, New York, 1961.

Bieber, H., "Technology transfer in practice," *IEEE Transactions on Engineering Management,* **EM-16**(4), p. 144, 1969.

Checkland, P. B., *Systems Thinking, Systems Practice,* John Wiley, New York, 1981.

Chernoff, H., and L. E. Moses, *Elementary Decision Theory,* John Wiley, New York, 1959.

Cleland, D. I., and H. Kerzner, *Project Management Dictionary of Terms,* Van Nostrand Reinhold, New York, 1985.

Fishburn, P. C., *Decision and Value Theory,* John Wiley, New York, 1964.

Hart, A. G., "Risk, uncertainty and the unprofitability of compounding probabilities," In O. Lange, F. McIntyre, and T. O. Yntema (eds.), *Studies in Mathematical Economics and Econometrics,* University of Chicago Press, 1941.

Miser, H. J., and E. S. Quade (eds.), *Systems Analysis,* John Wiley, New York, 1985.

Moore, J. R., "Technology transfer process between a large science-oriented and a large market-oriented company—The North American Rockwell challenge," *IEEE Transactions on Engineering Management,* **EM-16**(3), p. 111, 1969.

Niwa, K., M. Okuma, S. Seki, and I. Fujine, "Development of a risk alarm system for big construction projects," *Proc. of Project Management Institute Symposium,* p. 221, 1979.

Niwa, K., "Definition of risks," In *The Japan Society of Industrial Machinery Manufacturers, A Joint Study for Foreign Project Risk Management,* p. 25, 1981a.

Niwa, K., "Trouble library," in *The Japan Society of Industrial Machinery Manufacturers, A Joint Study for Foreign Project Risk Management,* p. 114, 1981b.

Quade, E. S., and W. I. Boucher (eds.), *Systems Analysis and Policy Planning: Application in Defense,* Elsevier, New York, 1968.

Rothwell, R., "Some problems of technology transfer into industry: Examples from the textile machinery sector," *IEEE Transactions on Engineering Management,* **EM-25**(1), p. 15, 1978.

Savage, L. J., *The Foundation of Statistics,* John Wiley, New York, 1954.

Stewart, J. M., "Techniques for technology transfer within the business firm," *IEEE Transactions on Engineering Management,* **EM-16**(3), p. 103, 1969.

Tintner, G., "A contribution to the non-static theory of production," In O. Lange, F. McIntyre, and T. O. Yntema (eds.), *Studies in Mathematical Economics and Econometrics,* University of Chicago Press, 1941.

Vaughan, E. J., *Fundamentals of Risk and Insurance,* Fourth Edition, John Wiley, New York, 1986.

Wideman, R. Max, *Cost Control of Capital Projects and the Project Cost Management System Requirements,* B.C.: AEW Services, Vancouver, 1983.

Wideman, R. Max. "Risk management." *Project Management Journal,* **17**(4), p. 20, 1986.

Williams, Jr., C. A., and R. M. Heins, *Risk Management and Insurance,* 5th ed., McGraw-Hill, New York, 1976.

SUGGESTIONS FOR DISCUSSION

1. Explain why risk definition of decision theory is too strict to apply to our problem.

2. What are the similarities and differences between construction projects and R&D projects in terms of risk management?

3. What are the advantages and disadvantages of "giving works only to experienced project managers" as a strategy for preventing risk recurrence?

4. Why is it generally difficult to transfer experience or knowledge of one project manager to other project managers?

5. If you were a project manager of large construction projects, how many different requirements of risk management systems could you list in addition to the four items described from (a) to (d)?

____3
EXPERT SYSTEMS

This chapter outlines expert systems because readers should understand the fundamental characteristics of expert systems before reading Chapters 4–6. These chapters describe how to develop an expert system in order to accomplish the required functions determined in Chapter 2.

Another purpose is to briefly present a perspective on the relationship between expert systems and human–computer cooperative systems. Special focus is on the general background of why and how human–computer cooperative systems will be invented for improving current expert systems. This may be helpful for readers because Chapters 6 and 7 identify the weak points of the expert system that is developed in Chapters 4–6, and discuss how to overcome them by human–computer cooperative systems.

This chapter is written from the methodological point of view. Therefore, it is a complement to the rest of the book, which is organized in the case study style in which human–computer cooperative systems are introduced primarily based on users' needs.

This chapter outlines expert systems and defines their fundamental characteristics. Next, some issues and limitations of current expert systems are presented in terms of these characteristics. Various approaches to overcoming such limitations will be discussed. Finally, possible strategies for future research in improving expert systems will be presented. Human–computer cooperative systems correspond to one of these strategies.

3.1 BRIEF OVERVIEW

Knowledge engineering, the art of AI that designs and builds expert systems (or knowledge-based systems), was first proposed in 1977 based on about 10 years of case studies in the fields of chemical analysis and medical diagnosis (Feigenbaum, 1977). The advent of knowledge engineering was one of the most important epochs in AI history, which started in the middle of the 1950s. The goal of AI scientists has been to determine what human intelligence is, or to develop computer programs that can solve problems as humans do (e.g., Barr and Feigenbaum, 1981, 1982; Cohen and Feigenbaum, 1982). Major research in AI before the emergence of knowledge engineering had concentrated on exploring "general" methods for problem solving, and for this reason was said to have produced no major breakthroughs. Knowledge engineering, on the other hand, paid special attention to domain specialists' knowledge and incorporated it into computer systems as knowledge bases for solving real-world problems. (Because a "domain specialist" is also considered an "expert," a system built by knowledge engineering is usually called an "expert system.")

An outline of an expert system is shown in Fig. 3.1. The purpose of expert systems is to help users solve real-world problems. Two key elements are a knowledge base consisting of domain specialists' knowledge and an inference engine. Pieces of domain specialists' knowledge are collected and stored in knowledge bases, as shown in Fig. 3.1. This procedure is called "knowledge acquisition."* Very typical examples with which such pieces of knowledge are stored in a knowledge base are:

If (the weather is fine) then (we go camping).

If (we go camping) then (we use the camping car).

This if–then form is one of the methods of storing knowledge called a "knowledge representation scheme."† The advantages of expert systems are that domain specialists' knowledge can easily be expressed by kowledge representation methods and can be stored in knowledge bases independently of inference engines that handle the knowledge. This permits easy implementation and maintenance of knowledge bases.

*Knowledge acquisition for our system is described in Chapter 4.

†More detailed overview of knowledge representation schemes, as well as that used in our system, is described in Chapter 5.

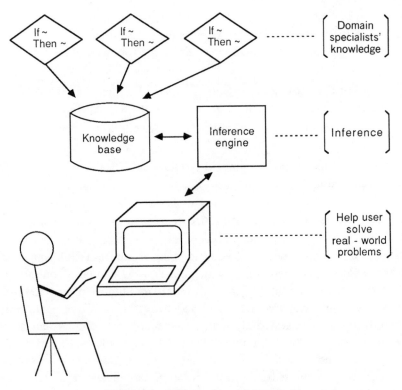

Figure 3.1. Outline of expert systems.

Inference engines search knowledge bases and logically combine pieces of knowledge when users want them. For example, the above two pieces of knowledge are combined and concluded as follows:

If (the weather is fine) then (we use the camping car).

This is done by "inference mechanisms" or just "inference," which is one of the methods of knowledge utilization.* Although there are many combinations of knowledge pieces in large knowledge bases, it is not necessary for inference engines to prepare as many procedures. Rather it is sufficient to prepare only a few basic procedures.† This is an advantage of expert systems associated with knowledge utilization. One the other hand, tradi-

*Inference and knowledge utilization of our system is discussed in Chapter 6.

†Examples are forward and backward reasoning procedures, which are discussed in Chapter 6.

tional computer systems that use algorithmic programming techniques usually have to clarify and prepare all possible procedures.

Expert systems may be characterized by the following three features:

- Use of the knowledge base that consists of domain specialists' knowledge (e.g., rules generated on the basis of their experience).
- Use of an inference mechanism that logically draws new conclusions from given facts.
- An attempt to solve real-world problems as effectively as domain specialists do.

Emphasis is usually placed on the first feature in order to attain the third feature. To solve real-world problems, expert systems have moved attentions to representing domain specialists' knowledge from exploring general inference or search methods on which old-type AI had been concentrated.

Although only about 10 years has passed, a number of expert systems have been built in many fields such as chemistry, medicine, engineering, manufacturing, business, and so on. The description of each system is omitted in this book because a number of excellent textbooks (e.g., Hayes-Roth, 1983; Waterman, 1986; Silverman, 1987) already address these subjects. Rather, we will discuss fundamental issues underlying expert systems in the next section, after having pointed out some shortcomings of current expert systems in the remainder of this section.

A variety of shortcomings of current expert systems have so far been addressed. Some of them are as follows:

(S1) Current expert systems can only be applied to very narrow domains.

(S2) It is not clear to what extent users may trust the answers that expert systems provide.

(S3) It is troublesome for users to have to respond to many awkward questions that expert systems address during reasoning processes. This is often mentioned as a typical problem caused by the lack of common sense of expert systems.

(S4) Effective methods of knowledge acquisition have not been developed.

(S5) Answers from expert systems are rather rigid compared with those of humans.

(S6) Some potential users do not want to use expert systems because this sometimes means showing a lack of expertise.

The next section clarifies and discusses the fundamental issues of current expert systems. These issues will be presented in accordance with the three features of expert systems that were pointed out in this section. In these discussions, including the preceding shortcomings (S1–S6) and some approaches to overcoming them involving a new approach, a human–computer cooperative system.

3.2 ISSUES IN CURRENT EXPERT SYSTEMS

3.2.1 Issues in the Use of Domain Specialists' Knowledge

The first feature of expert systems is the "use of domain specialists' knowledge," which implies the following three subfeatures:

1. Domain specialists' knowledge should be concentrated on rather than human common sense.
2. Domain specialists' knowledge generally covers a narrow field.
3. Knowledge acquisition (sometimes called knowledge elicitation) from domain specialists (sometimes called experts or knowledge suppliers) is necessary.

With respect to subfeature 1, we should refrain from only saying that "one of the disadvantages of current expert systems is derived from the defect of common sense." (This corresponds to shortcoming S3.) Instead, issues that should be discussed are:

- Which domains can be effectively applied by expert systems that contain only domain specialists' knowledge?
- If common sense is necessary for "effective" expert systems, how much or what kind of common sense is necessary, and is this so large as to prevent the first feature of expert systems?

It is assumed that expert systems mainly use domain specialists' knowledge, although human intuitive ability (strictly speaking, intuitive ability is different from common sense) is included in our human–computer cooperative system to overcome weak points of current expert systems.

The issue regarding to subfeature 2 may be how large fields can be in which "effective" expert systems can be developed and in which specialists' knowledge can be acquired. Fields requiring multiple knowledge of existing disciplines are promising. (This is one of the approaches to overcome shortcoming S1.) In these fields there is certainly need for knowledge because not everyone can be an expert in multiple disciplines. The difficulties of knowledge acquisition in such fields in of roughly the same order as in a single discipline, if knowledge can be acquired from various discipline experts and successfully incorporated into a knowledge base. Large-project management may be regarded as one of the most typical fields that has the above characteristics (Niwa and Okuma, 1982; Niwa and Sasaki, 1983) and will be treated in this book as a case study.

Knowledge acquisition subfeature 3 may be the biggest problem of knowledge engineering. (See, e.g., Knowledge acquisition for knowledge-based system. Parts 1–3, special issue of *International Journal of Man–Machine Studies,* **26,** 1987.) In addition to various studies (e.g., exploring knowledge representation that helps easy knowledge acqusition, developing efficient maintenance tools for a knowledge base, and implementing efficient user interfaces), we point out here the importance of cognitive psychology and organizational design approaches. For example, we should develop methods that help knowledge suppliers remember and express their experience, and we should establish organizational procedures that encourage them to provide their knowledge.* (These may be the approaches to overcome shortcoming S4.)

The fundamental problem underlying all the subfeatures is that we have virtually no means of scientifically verifying the validity of domain specialists' knowlege. (This corresponds to shortcoming S2.) There are two types of domain specialists' knowledge: scientific knowledge that appears in textbooks and experimental knowledge obtained through experience. A major goal of expert systems has been to handle the latter knowledge. It should be determined which fields are appropriate to expert systems that contain experimental knowledge (and not scientific knowledge). We think management fields are promising because problem solving and decision making are carried out largely based on managers' knowledge obtained through experience. The case study in this book (i.e., project risk management) deals with the management fields.

---

*Some approaches taken for these purposes in our system are described in Chapter 8.

3.2.2 Issues in the Use of Inference Mechanisms

The second feature of expert systems is the use of inference mechanisms. A simple example is that both (A) and (If A then B) result in (B). The inference process is logical or, in a sense, "mechanical." This results in the answers from expert systems being within the set that consists of initial knowledge and knowledge that is obtained by the inference processes. (This corresponds to shortcoming S5.) On the contrary, human experts, unlike expert systems, do not always reason by using inference mechanisms (e.g., Dreyfus and Dreyfus, 1986). Therefore, issues to be discussed are:

1. Which fields are appropriate to expert systems even if they have the above limitation?
2. How can we overcome the limitation?

With regard to item 1, the following two viewpoints may be presented:

1a. There may be many fields where expert systems can be used as "knowledge retrieval systems," the function of which is to search knowledge bases by using logical inference in addition to the usual retrieval methods. However, a prerequisite of this is that the knowledge base must contain very large amounts of knowledge. This prerequisite may contradict the common maxim for building expert systems, "Focus on a narrow speciality area" (e.g., Hayes-Roth, 1983). This maxim may be for pilot systems of beginners because it is technically easy to develop expert systems for narrow areas. Expert systems that contain only narrow and small amounts of knowledge will soon become obsolete. (This corresponds to shortcoming S1.)

1b. Natural science or engineering fields may be appropriate for expert systems because these fields have been established by inference mechanisms using scientific knowledge. Typical samples are expert systems for failure diagnosis of digital circuits, mechanical machines, or chemical plants. The expert system knowledge bases store knowledge concerning domain structures and functions, which are mainly involved in design drawings or scientific knowlege. These expert systems provide a variety of output, even though it is derived only from inference processes. This idea corresponds to the "model approach" or the "deep-knowledge approach" (David et al., 1982; Hart, 1982; Michie, 1982). However, the disadvantage of this approach is it resembles the traditional scientific methods used in existing science and engineering disciplines.

Much research on item 2 is under way. Some of it involve research on parallel distributing processing (Rumelhart et al, 1986; McClelland et al, 1986) and neural networks (Hopfield, 1982; Hopfield and Tank, 1986). These methods are "microscopic" approaches since they focus on interactions of lare numbers of simple processing units that may correspond to neurons. They are unifying neuroscience and cognitive science in a computational framework so that models of basic aspects of perception, memory, language, and thought may be developed. However, more research and breakthroughs are necessary to apply these methods to such "macroscopic" real-world problems as current expert systems handle. On the other hand, the human–computer cooperative sytsem is a "macroscopic" approach toward achieving item 2 for real-world problem solving since the overall human intuitive process is considered, as will be discussed in Chapters 6 and 7.

3.2.3 Issues in the Attempt to Solve Real-World Problems

The third feature of expert systems is the attempt to solve real-world problems. However, it should be noticed that computer systems for management are not always used, even if they are technically good systems. In the management science fields, the importance of this fact was pointed out in the late 1960s (Churchman, 1965), and for the past 20 years, research on the implementation of management science and information systems has occurred. This is called "implementation research" or "implementation theory" (e.g., Doctor et al., 1979; Schultz, 1987). Implementation research has shown that many factors affect the practical use of systems. For example, member constitutions of system development projects (whether they involve users, top management, system development engineers, or research staffs) and decision-making styles of users have strong influences on the success of system implementations. One important point we should learn from implementation research is that there is a big difference between demonstration systems in laboratories and practical systems in the real world, and this difference is not always derived from technical aspects but rather from organizational or managerial aspects. (This corresponds to shortcoming S6.)

In addition to the implementation research on traditional information systems, in the remainder of this section we will present our new viewpoint (Niwa, 1988a) which is unique to knowledge-based systems.

For successful application of knowledge-based systems, it has been generally said that efficient Technology Transfer (TT) of AI technologies to such systems is critical. This seems reasonable, because TT means the flow of new technologies from research to production, or from research to practical application (e.g., Bieber, 1969; Rothwell, 1978; Boyle, 1986). However, the primary concern of knowledge-based system users should be whether the systems can provide useful knowledge for efficient problem solving, and not merely whether such systems contain new AI technologies. Therefore, we should pay more attention to "knowledge transfer" (KT) as a key to the successful application of knowledge-based systems. Knowledge transfer is defined as the flow of knowledge from knowledge suppliers (through knowledge-based systems) to users. The relationship between TT and KT for knowledge-based systems is shown in Fig. 3.2. TT flows from the bottom to the top, whereas KT flows form the left to the right.

The importance of KT has escaped the notice of people in virtually all categories of the knowledge/technology flow diagrammed in Fig. 3.2. Some of the reasons for this are as follows (Niwa, 1988a):

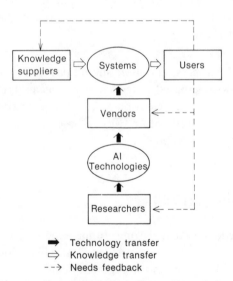

➡   Technology transfer
⇨   Knowledge transfer
--→ Needs feedback

Figure 3.2. Relation between technology transfer and knowledge transfer in the field of knowledge-based systems. (From Niwa, 1988a. Reprinted with permission from Cambridge University Press.)

- Most knowledge-based systems have remained at the demonstration or experimental level. Potential users do not request real knowledge from such systems. Thus, there is no need for feedback regarding knowledge from users to vendors or researchers. As a result, system vendors and developers do not become aware of the importance of the knowledge itself. Instead, they concentrate their efforts on developing tools that support easy implementation of "demonstration" systems.

- Some successful systems, although very few, have been developed by excellent researchers and developers who are experts in both AI technologies and domain knowledge. As a result, AI technologies and domain knowledge are so well incorporated into knowledge-based systems that users do not explicitly recognize the important role of knowledge. Rather, they are apt to think that the good system performance is due mainly to the vendor technologies. From their business point of view, this is what the vendors wish the users to understand.

- Researchers and developers are apt to concentrate on technology transfer aspects and not on knowledge transfer aspects. This is largely because knowledge transfer aspects cannot always be handled by current AI technologies, and using old fashioned technologies (not AI technologies) is not regarded by AI professionals as producing achievements.

Researchers, developers, and users should pay more attention to KT aspects so that knowledge-based systems may emerge in practice. Some other lessons for successful implementation of knolwedge-based systems obtained during our 10 years of R&D of knowledge-based project risk management systems is presented in Chapter 8.

3.3   FUTURE DIRECTIONS

The previous section discussed some fundamental issues involved in the three features that characterize expert systems. This section presents some possible future R&D strategies for expert systems.

The current status of AI owes a great deal to the advent of "expert systems" (Feigenbaum, 1977). Many great achievements have resulted from using expert systems. Some of these achievements are:

- Expert systems have improved software-engineering performance (e.g., programming productivity and program maintainability) by providing programming styles that permit high-modularity representation of knowledge and that separate knowledge bases from inference engines.
- Expert systems allow us to pay more attention to the importance of knowledge obtained through experience, an idea that is accurately expressed as "power is knowledge" (Feigenbaum, 1977; Lenat and Feigenbaum, 1987). In the coming information-intensive society, domain specialists' knowledge obtained through experience will become one of the most valuable competitive resources in various fields because scientific knowledge or knowledge appearing in standard textbooks is easily accessible through information networks and various data bases.
- Expert systems have been influential in many students' decision to work in the AI fields. This certainly contributes to the future of AI.

In spite of these achievements, we must admit that expert systems have not so far succeeded in answering the original question of AI (i.e., what human intelligence is). It is important for researchers and developers of expert systems not to forget this original question of AI, as well as not to exaggerate the "potential" of expert systems, so that expert systems (or knowledge-based systems) can be sufficiently developed.

It is true that AI people are researching human intelligence by using computer techniques; however, the following equation often appears in their conversation:

$$(\text{Human}) - (\text{AI}) = (\text{Intelligence})$$

What is the meaning of this equation? One possible answer is to assume that since "intelligence" means what we cannot understand by existing methods, if we can understand a part of human and formalize it as AI, this part no longer is called intelligence. In this way, the equation may represent a very reasonable idea: scientists reveal secrets of intelligence step by step. However, a problem reamins if (Human) $= \infty$. Another possible answer is to assume that current AI research does not directly address the essence of intelligence, as correctly expressed by the above equation. Some people (e.g., Dreyfus, 1965; Dreyfus, 1972; Dreyfus and Dreyfus, 1986; Weizenbaum, 1976) presented doubts about AI from this second viewpoint.

As mentioned above, AI research may be difficult and uncertain. However, for this reason, it certainly arouses interest. There may be many strategies for future research, which involve the following three alternatives:

1. *Analytic Strategy.* To explore the essence of intelligence, research elemental areas of expert systems involving answers to such questions as, Do such elemental fields exist? How can we identify them? Do researches contribute to expert system development? How can we integrate the results of such research into expert systems? A variety of interactions among physiology, psychology, linguistics, logic, and system science may be a key to this strategy.

2. *Improvement Strategy.* Repeat the cycle of system development, usage, and improvement until system performance reaches a workable level in the real world (i.e., until users are satisfied with the system). Although it is extremely difficult to reach such a level, it may be possible for us to identify or discover research themes relevant to exploring human intelligence by repeating the above cycle. When pursuing this strategy, we should take care not to concentrate on only improving the computer environment (hardware and software) if that is merely the method of research. Rather we should improve the ideas or concepts that are substantial working hypotheses for approaching human intelligence.

3. *Goal-Oriented Strategy.* First identify desirable relationships between humans and future intelligent computers; in other words, identify the functions that future humans will want intelligent computers to perform, although this is very difficult. Then direct our research activities toward achieving these functions. In identifying and achieving such functions, consider the differences between computers and humans, which is directly related to human intelligence.

The improvement strategy is used in Chapters 4–6. However, the goal-oriented strategy is applied in Chapter 7, in which a human–computer cooperative system is a goal.

3.4 SUMMARY

The historical background and outline of expert systems were briefly described and three fundamental characteristics of expert systems were identified. These characteristics were use of a knowledge base that consists of domain specialists' knowledge, use of an inference mechanism, and an attempt to solve real-world problems. Then issues involved in current expert systems were discussed in terms of these three characteristics. Some of these issues were which domains can be effectively applied to expert systems, how the inference limitation can be overcome, and how systems can actually be used. Approaches to overcome such issues were multiple discipline management domains, human–computer cooperations with large knowledge bases, and taking care of organizational aspects. Finally, three possible strategies for future research of expert systems were discussed. These were an analytic strategy, an improvement strategy, and a goal-oriented strategy. The human–computer cooperative system corresponds to the goal-oriented strategy.

REFERENCES

Barr, A., and E. A. Feigenbaum, *The Handbook of Artificial Intelligence,* Vol. 1, William Kaufmann, Los Altos, CA, 1981.

Barr, A., and E. A. Feigenbaum, *The Handbook of Artificial Intelligence,* Vol. 2, William Kaufmann, Los Altos, CA, 1982.

Bieber, H., "Technology transfer in practice," *IEEE Transactions on Engineering Management,* **EM-16**(4), p. 144, 1969.

Boyle, K. A., "Technology transfer between universities and the U.K. offshore industry," *IEEE Transactions on Engineering Management,* **EM-33**(1), p. 33, 1986.

Churchman, C. W., and A. H. Schainblatt, "The researcher and the manager—A dialect of implementation," *Management Science,* **11,** p. B69, 1965.

Cohen, P. R., and E. A. Feigenbaum, *The Handbook of Artificial Intelligence,* Vol. 3, William Kaufmann, Los Altos, CA, 1982.

Davis, R., H. Shrobe, W. Hamscher, K. Wieckert, M. Shirley, and S. Polit, "Diagnosis based on structure and function," *Proc. of American Association for Artificial Intelligence National Conference,* p. 137, 1982.

Doctor, R., R. L. Schultz, and D. P. Slevin (eds.), *The Implementation of Management Science,* In R. Machol (ed.), TIMS Studies in the Management Sciences 13, North-Holland, New York, 1979.

Dreyfus, H. L., "Alchemy and artificial intelligence," *The RAND Corporation Paper P-3244,* 1965.

Dreyfus, H. L., *What Computers Can't Do: The Limits of Artificial Intelligence,* Harper and Row, 1972.

Dreyfus, H. L., and S. E. Dreyfus, *Mind Over Machine,* Free Press, New York, 1986.

Feigenbaum, E. A., "The art of artificial intelligence. I. Themes and case studies of knowledge engineering," *Proc. of Fifth International Joint Conference on Artificial Intelligence,* p. 1014, 1977.

Hart, P. E., "Direction for AI in the eighties," *SIGART,* **79,** p. 11, 1982.

Hayes-Roth, F., D. A. Waterman, and D. B. Lenat (eds.), *Bulling Expert Systems,* Addison-Wesley, Reading, MA, 1983.

Hopfield, J. J., "Neural networks and physical systems with emergent collective computational abilities," *Proc. of National Academy of Science USA,* **79,** p. 2554, 1982.

Hopfield, J. J., and D. W. Tank, "Computing with neural circuits: A model," *Science,* **233,** p. 625, 1986.

Lenat, D. B., and E. A. Feigenbaum, "On the thresholds of knowledge," *Proc. of Tenth International Joint Conference on Artificial Intelligence,* p. 1173, 1987.

McClelland, J. L., D. E. Rumelhart, and the PDP Research Group, *Parallel Distributed Processing: Explorations in the Microstructure of Cognition, Volume 2, Psychological and Biological Models,* MIT Press, Cambridge, MA, 1986.

Michie, D., "High-road and low-road programs," *AI Magazine,* **3**(1), p. 21, 1982.

Niwa, K., and M. Okuma, "Know-how transfer method and its application to risk management for large construction projects," *IEEE Transactions on Engineering Management,* **EM-29**(4), p. 146, 1982.

Niwa, K., and K. Sasaki, "A new project management system approach: The know-how based project management system," *Project Management Quarterly,* **14**(1), p. 65, 1983.

Niwa, K., "Knowledge transfer: A key to successful application of knowledge-based sytems," *The Knowledge Engineering Review,* **2**(2), p. 145, 1988a.

Rothwell, R., "Some problems of technology transfer into industry: Examples from the textile machinery sector," *IEEE Transactions on Engineering Management,* **EM-25**(1), p. 15, 1978.

Rumelhart, D. E., J. L. McClelland, and the PDP Research Group, *Parallel Distributed Processing: Explorations in the Microstructure of Cognition,* Volume 1, Foundation, MIT Press, Cambridge, MA, 1986.

Schultz, R. L., Special Issue, "Implementation," *Interface* **17**(3), 1987.

Silverman, B. G. (ed.), *Expert Systems for Business,* Addison-Wesley, Reading, MA, 1987.

Waterman, D. A., *A Guide To Expert Systems,* Addison-Wesley, Reading, MA, 1986.

Weizenbaum, J., *Computer Power and Human Reason: From Judgment to Calculation,* Freeman, New York, 1976.

SUGGESTIONS FOR DISCUSSION

1. What is the impact of the advent of expert systems on AI fields?

2. Give example domains which can be applied by expert systems that contain domain specialists' knowledge.

3. It has been suggested that expert systems will apply to fields that require multiple knowledge of existing domains. Explain why you agree or disagree.

4. Discuss the problem of our having virtually no means to scientifically verify the validity of domain specialists' knowledge.

5. Explain and illustrate by example what is meant by inference.

6. Why is KT (knowledge transfer) important for successful application of knowledge-based systems?

7. Discuss the equation:

$$(\text{Human}) - (\text{AI}) = (\text{Intelligence})$$

8. Discuss the advantages and disadvantages of the following three strategies for future research on AI:

   - Analytic strategy
   - Improvement strategy, and
   - Goal-oriented strategy

9. Which one of the above three strategies (or another strategy) will you choose? Why?

10. Explain the relationship between current expert systems and human–computer cooperative systems.

4

KNOWLEDGE ACQUISITION

This chapter presents the methods and procedures for acquiring knowledge, as well as knowledge that is actually obtained. According to the requirement analysis in Chapter 2, the scope of knowledge to be stored in the knowledge base is identified in Section 4.1. A "risk mechanism model" and a "standard work package method" is developed and used for this purpose.

Next, actual procedures for acquiring this knowledge is presented. Although knowledge acquisition is recognized as a very critical step in the development of knowledge-based systems, little has been published on actual cases. Therefore, actual experience with this procedure is described. (Related discussions appear from different viewpoints in Chapter 8.) Finally, some examples of knowledge that has actually been acquired is demonstrated.

4.1 ANALYSIS OF DOMAIN KNOWLEDGE

The purpose of this section is to determine the scope of knowledge that will be acquired and stored in the knowledge base. A guideline should correspond to the four system requirements presented in Fig. 2.4 of Chapter 2. According to the third requirement (to analyze cause and risk mechanisms), a risk mechanism model should be constructed that will identify the risk-related knowledge that should be acquired. The first (to collect a large amount of experience) and the second (to be adaptable to many construction projects) requirements lead the discussion of a standard work package method, which acts as a mapping tool between risks and work elements of projects. This method will also identify the kinds of knowledge or data that should be collected. The fourth requirement, improved abilities, is discussed in more detail in Chapters 6 and 7.

4.1.1 Risk Mechanism Model

If a risk mechanism model that explains risk causality based on actual risk cases can be constructed and incorporated into project risk management systems, it will be very effective in informing project managers of risks in advance (i.e., the third system requirement in Fig. 2.4). By using this model it will be possible for project managers to prevent the recurrence of similar risks.

Risks were collected from various departments in large engineering companies and analyzed to construct a risk mechanism model. The risk mechanism model that was developed is shown in Fig. 4.1. The mechanism is as follows:

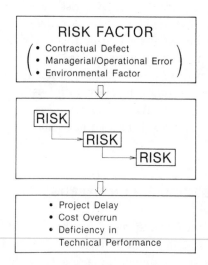

Figure 4.1. Risk mechanism mode. (From Niwa, 1979. Reprinted with permission of the Project Management Institute, P.O. Box 43, Drexel Hill, PA.)

- A risk has causes that will be called "risk factors." These risk factors are classified into three categories: contractual defects, managerial or operational errors, and environmental factors.
- Some risks may bring about other risks, called "consequent risks," if no risk-reducing strategies are used.
- A risk brings project delays, cost overruns, or deficiencies in technical performance, which is the definition of risks determined in Section 2.1.

In Fig. 4.1, risk factors play an important role. If project managers can notice or observe risk factors during projects, they may enter these risk factors into the risk mechanism model so that they can be informed of the potential risks. Therefore, it is necessary for us to identify and determine the extent of the risk factors. By analyzing a variety of actual risk cases that were collected as well as by researching published resources (e.g., newspapers), we have determined and fixed the extent of risk factors as including (1) contractual defects, (2) managerial and operational errors, and (3) environmental factors. Some examples of individual items that we have identified in these three categories will be presented in Section 4.3.

4.1.2 Standard Work Package Method

As a mapping tool between risks and project work elements, we will present a standard work package method (Niwa and Okuma, 1982). This method is designed to achieve the second system requirement of managers (i.e., being able to recognize risks that correspond to the size of the work element they want), as shown in Fig. 2.4. This method will be explained conceptually and formally (i.e., mathematically). Those who are not interested in the formal explanation can skip this second part.

The heart of the idea—standard work package method—is diagrammed in Fig. 4.2. There are two matrices in the figure, each of which is a standard work package matrix. The horizontal axis represents project activities such as engineering, procurement, installation, and so on. The vertical axis represents objects (equipment or buildings) of activities such as boiler, turbine, condenser of thermal power plant. The lower matrix shows that any work element, called a "work package," of a certain project can be defined in the standard work pacakge matrix by framing its area. For example, work package w_1 is defined by activities a_1 and a_2 and by objects o_1 and o_2.

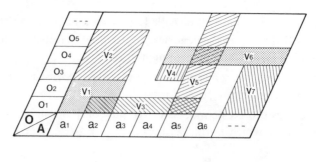

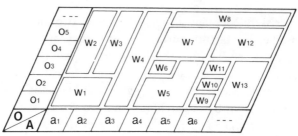

Figure 4.2. Standard work package method.

$A = \{a_i\}$: Activity, $O = \{o_i\}$: Object, $W = \{w_i\}$: Work package,
$V = \{v_i\}$: The domain to which knowledge k_i corresponds.

The upper matrix shows how a number of pieces of knowledge are related to the domain in the matrix. A piece of knowledge k_3, for example, is related to the area v_3 and is defined by activities a_2, a_3, a_4, and a_5, and by object o_1. In the project risk managemet field, this situation can be interpreted as risk k_3 occurring in project domain v_3.

By superimposing the two matrices, it is easy to obtain knowledge related to a certain work package in a project, and *vice versa*. For example, pieces of knowledge relating to work package w_1 are k_1 and k_3. This is because the area w_1 overlaps areas v_1 and v_3, and because v_1 and v_3 correspond to k_1 and k_3, respectively. In the same way, work packages relating to knowledge k_3 are w_1, w_4, and w_5.

The advantage of the standard work package method can be summarized as follows: if activities and objects can be identified so that a standard work package matrix may be developed, a great variety of knowledge of many projects can be stored in this matrix independently of the work packages of certain projects. Any piece of knowledge can then be extracted that is related to a certain work package of any project. Consequently, the standard work package method achieves the second system requirement of being able to recognize risks that correspond to any size of the work package.

In this way, the knowledge and data necessary to fulfill the second requirement of the system are determined: project activities, objects (equipment or buildings) of activities, and the domains (defined by the pair of activities and objects) that correspond to each risk. These examples are presented in Section 4.3.

A brief discussion about the differences between a work breakdown structure (WBS) (NASA, 1975) and the standard work package matrix has been added because WBS is a very common tool in the project management field (e.g., Cleland and King, 1983) and also because it resembles the standard work package matrix. A WBS is a family tree subdivision of the efforts that are required to achieve an end goal. The emphasis of WBS is to diagram the relationships between means and goals, or systems and elements in a project. On the other hand, the main purpose of the standard work package matrix is to show the scope of a project by two explicit parameters: activity and object. Special attention is paid to repeatable characteristics in construction projects, which R&D projects usually do not have. This leads to the idea of a standard as a mapping tool between knowledge and work packages in construction projects. Attention is also given to the fact that the knowledge domain is defined by either or both activities and objects. Although knowledge in many cases corresponds to a certain work package that is defined both by activity and by object, it sometimes corresponds to only one element. For instance, some knowledge about customs clearance can be applied to all objects. This means that the application domain of this knowledge can be defined by activity without information about objects. This cannot be easily expressed by the tree structure of WBS. Therefore clear indication of both activities and objects (i.e., matrix structure) is useful for construction projects.

The remainder of this section explains the standard work package method more formally (Niwa and Okuma, 1982). Therefore, those who are not interested in a formal explanation can skip to the next section.

The fundamental variables that determine the scope of construction projects are activities and objects. Sets of activities and objects are represented as follows:
Activity Set

$$A = \{a_1, a_2, \ldots, a_l\}. \tag{4.1}$$

Object Set

$$O = \{o_1, o_2, \ldots, o_m\}. \tag{4.2}$$

Each element in the project, w_i, called a "work package," can be expressed as a subset of the direct product of A and O.
Work package

$$w_i \subseteq A \times O, \tag{4.3}$$

where

$$w_i \cap w_j = \varnothing, \, i \neq j, \, i, j \, \epsilon \, (1, 2, \ldots, p), \, p \leq lm.$$

For example,
Activity set for thermal power station construction project:

$$A = \{a_1, a_2, a_3, \ldots\}$$
$$= \{\textit{engineering, manufacturing, transportation, } \ldots\}.$$

Object set for thermal power station construction project:

$$O = \{o_1, o_2, o_3, \ldots\}$$
$$= \{\textit{boiler, turbine, generator, } \ldots\}.$$

Work package for engineering of a boiler:

$$w_1 = \{a_1, o_1\}.$$

Work package for transporting a boiler and turbine:

$$w_5 = \{(a_3, o_1), (a_3, o_2)\}.$$

Knowledge related to the project can be treated as follows:
Knowledge Set

$$K = \{k_1, k_2, \ldots, k_n\}. \tag{4.4}$$

Let v_j be defined as the domain of work to which knowledge k_j corresponds:

$$v_j = f(k_j). \tag{4.5}$$

v_j is then a member of the next set V.

$$V = \{v_j \mid v_j \subseteq A \times O\}. \tag{4.6}$$

Therefore, the set of knowledge that corresponds to the work package w_i is

$$K(w_i) = \{k_j \mid w_i \cap v_j \neq \varnothing, j = 1, 2, \ldots, n\}, \tag{4.7}$$

and the set of work packages that corresponds to the knowledge k_i is

$$W(k_i) = \{w_j \mid v_i \cap w_j \neq \varnothing, j = 1, 2, \ldots, p, p \leq lm\} \tag{4.8}$$

4.2   KNOWLEDGE ACQUISITION PROCEDURES

This section describes the knowledge acquisition procedures that are used to develop a project risk management system or, more specifically, a knowledge-based system for risk management of power plant (thermal, gas turbine, and substation) construction projects. Based on the "risk mechanism model" (Fig. 4.1) and the "standard work package method" (Fig. 4.2), two categories of items that are entered into the knowledge base have been classified.

The items in the first category should be determined before the items in the second category are collected. They are activities of thermal power construction projects, objects (equipment or buildings) of such activities, contractual defect risk factors, operational/managerial error risk factors, and environmental risk factors. To identify these items, a task force team was organized that consisted of senior project managers and systems scientists (including the author). The most important point to which the team paid special attention was the consistency between items to be identified and items used widely in the company. This assures efficient application of an existing large body of knowledge to the project risk management system. Such existing knowledge involves project check lists, equipment item lists, contract manuals, classification codes for accident reports, and site survey item lists. Also, consistency will assure the integrated use of existing project control systems (e.g., cost control or schedule control systems) with the project risk management system. Examples of items that have been identified are presented in the next section.

The items in the second category are those directly related to risks and risk-reducing strategies, although we will only focus on risks in this book. Both the risk mechanism model and the standard work package method have determined the scope of knowledge and data to be collected from project managers and project members. These involve risks, their work packages (i.e., pairs of activities and objects) where these risks happened, their risk factors, and their consequent risks. (Risk-reducing strategies and work packages where these strategies are used are beyond the scope of this book.)

The items in the second category have been collected by two methods. One method was interviewing "established" or "top class" project managers, as shown in Fig. 4.3. When they were asked, they were usually pleased to tell about risks that had actually happened in their projects, where (work packages) and why (risk factors) they happened, and so on. Little difficulty was experienced in interviewing them largely because they thought that knowledge transfer was one of the responsibilities of established or top class project managers, and also because they were too well established to be damaged by the disclosure of their risk experiences. In almost all cases, the obtained knowledge was very informative and useful for other project managers and personnel. Moreover, we could perform such interviews very efficiently, since we could ask them about any ambiguities.

In spite of the great advantages of this interview method for knowledge

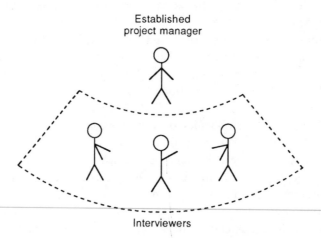

Figure 4.3. Knowledge acquisition method 1: interview with established project managers.

acquisition, we could not rely entirely upon it because there were only a few established or top class project managers. Therefore, in addition to this interview method, questionnaires were used. An outline of this method is shown in Fig. 4.4. Questionnaires were distributed to all the project managers and major project members who had just finished projects. Sometimes it is better to gather questionnaires continuously (e.g., every month or every two weeks) because most recent projects have been very long term. Questionnaires for this study were gathered every month. Each collected questionnaire was carefully examined in group meetings for about 20 minutes. Every group consisted of three senior project managers or project personnel whose careers were different. They checked for errors or mistakes in the questionnaires, and if necessary, some were returned to writers to clarify ambiguities. The most important role of this group meeting was to complement or add knowledge to each questionnaire from various viewpoints. For example, topics of the group meetings included the following:

- Are expressions of risk clear?
- Are there other possible risk factors that bring about this risk?
- Are there other possible work packages where this risk may occur?
- Are there other possible consequent risks?

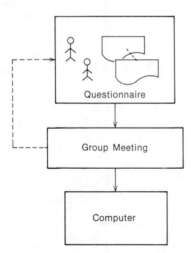

Figure 4.4. Knowledge acquisition method 2: questionnaires (From Niwa, 1979. Reprinted with permission of The Project Management Institute, P.O. Box 43, Drexel Hill, PA.)

Some examples of the items obtained through interviews or questionnaires will be demonstrated in the next section. They will be stored in a knowledge base by the technique described in Chapter 5.

4.3 OBTAINED KNOWLEDGE

A part of a major activity list of power plant construction projects (thermal power plants, gas turbine plants, and substation plants) for project risk management is shown in Fig. 4.5. The first hierarchical level includes such activities as proposal preparation, contract and engineering, producion and procurement, transportation and dispatch, civil work, installation, trial running, operation and return home, receipt money and remittance, and others. These activities are divided into several items in the second hierarchical level. Installation, for example, is divided into such activities as site storage, preparation of temporary facilities, carrying, welding, assembling and piping, parts check, and cleanup. This list is slightly different from the

CODE	ACTIVITY	CODE	ACTIVITY
0.	Proposal preparation	4.	Civil work
01.	Previous survey		
02.	Estimation	5.	Installation
1.	Contract & engineering	51.	Installation
		5101	Site storage
11.	Contract	5102	Temporary facilities
2.	Production & procurement	5103	Carrying
		5104	Welding
		5105	Assembling, wiring & piping
3.	Transportation & dispatch	5106	Part check
		5107	Clean up
31.	Transportation		
3101	Customs clearance	6.	Trial running
32.	Supervisor dispatch		
3201	Departure	7.	Operation & return home
3202	Passage	71.	Operation
3203	Entry	7101	Operation during guarantee period
3204	Leave for new post	7102	

Figure 4.5. Activities of power plant construction projects.

CODE	RISK FACTOR	CODE	RISK FACTOR
3A..	Climate	3G..	Labor
3A01	Severe climate condition	3G01	Difference in work customs
3A02	Severe change of seasons	3G02	Lack of worker ability
3B..	Calamity	3G03	Shortage of labor
3C..	Site condition	3G04	Strike or sabotage by workers
		3H..	Local company
3D..	Disease	3I..	Economics
3E..	Infrastructure	3I01	Inflation
3E01	Port congestion	3J..	Politics
3E02	Deficiency of harbor facility	3J01	Uneasiness of political conditions
3F..	Utility	3J02	Military activity

Figure 4.8. Risk factors: environmental factors.

A risk knowledge example is shown in Fig. 4.9. The first risk, 3104001, for example, is "equipment damage due to shaking during transportation." The work package where this risk occurred is defined by inland transportation activity and all equipment, as shown in the figure. (The activity of all the risks in Fig. 4.9 is inland transportation, as shown in the headline "risk in inland transportation".) The risk factors of this risk are 2F37 (insufficient) precautions of construction department) for managerial/operational errors, and 3B01 (bad weather) and 3E07 (bad road conditions), both of which are environmental factors. Another risk, 3104003, is shown to have many equipment codes such as G1B (generator and accessory of gas turbine plant), SD (transformer of substation plant), T1B (drum, header, and pressure parts of boiler of thermal plant), and so on. This means that the work packages where this risk occurred (and also may occur) are those defined by these objects and inland transportation activity.

4.4 SUMMARY

This chapter discussed knowledge acquisition for project risk management of large construction projects. To determine the scope of the knowledge

CODE	RISK IN INLAND TRANSPORTATION	EQUIPMENT	RISK FACTOR		
			C.D.	M/O.E.	E.F.
3104001	Equipment damage due to shaking during transportation	ALL		2F37	3B01 3E07
3104002	Equipment damage due to bad handling by local labor	ALL		2F37	3E07 3G02
3104003	Goods overturn during train shipment	G1B SD T1B T1I T2B T2C T2D T2F T3B T3C T3D T3E		2D37	3E04
3104004	Equipment falls due to wire slip of wrecker	ALL		2E37	3G02
3104005	Transportation delay due to incomplete documents	ALL	1B03	2E37	3M01 3Q01
3104006	Restricted transportation due to regulations change	ALL	1E02	2H37	3K02
3104007	Impossible to sail river due to unusual drought	ALL		2H37	3A02 3B01
3104008	Road damage due to heavy equipment transportation	G1B SD T1B T1I T2B T2C T2D		2F37 2H37	3E07

Figure 4.9 Risk knowledge example. C.D.: contractual defects; M/O.E.: managerial/operational errors; E.F.: environmental factors.

that should be acquired and stored in the knowledge base, domain knowledge was analyzed and a risk mechanism model as well as a standard work package method were developed based on the system requirements determined in Chapter 2.

The risk mechanism model was developed to explain the relationship (i.e., risk causality) among risk factors, risks, and consequent risks. Risk factors, defined as causes of risks, were classified into contractual defects, managerial/operational errors, and environmental factors. In this way, it became clear that these items have to be identified and stored in the system. Incorporating this model into the project management system allows project managers to be informed of risks in advance.

The standard work package method was developed to enable the transfer of risk knowledge from a certain project to other projects by mapping the risks to the standard work package matrix. (A work package was defined as a pair consisting of project activities and their objects.) In this way, it became clear that one must collect risk experiences together with the work packages in which they occurred.

Next methods actually used in acquiring the above knowledge were described. Interviews with established or top class project managers were very effective in acquiring risk knowledge, although there were few such project managers. Therefore, in addition to these, questionnaires were distributed to a number of project managers and project personnel to collect risk experiences. Four or five group meetings, each consisting of three senior project managers, were organized to correct ambiguities as well as to complement or add knowledge.

Finally, some examples of this acquired knowledge was demonstrated. This knowledge will be stored in a computer by using a technique described in Chapter 5.

REFERENCES

Cleland, D. I., and W. R. King (eds.), *Project Management Handbook,* Van Nostrand Reinhold, New York, 1983.

NASA (National Aeronautics and Space Administration), *Handbook for Preparation of Work Breakdown Structure,* NHB 5610.1, February 1975.

Niwa, K., and M. Okuma, "Know-how transfer method and its application to risk management for large construction projects," *IEEE Transactions on Engineering Management,* **EM-29**(4), p. 146, 1982.

SUGGESTIONS FOR DISCUSSION

1. If you were a project manager, how would you use the risk mechanism model shown in Fig. 4.1?

2. Using Fig. 4.2, explain why a great variety of knowledge of many projects can be stored *independently* of certain projects.

3. Discuss the advantages and disadvantages of these knowledge acquisition methods:

   • Interviews with established project managers, and
   • Questionnaire method

4. Why is knowledge acquisition generally difficult?

5. How many different ways can you list that will be used for effective knowledge acquisition?

___5
KNOWLEDGE REPRESENTATION

This chapter discusses "knowledge representation": how the knowledge acquired in Chapter 4 is stored in the knowledge base. Since there have been various methods for representing knowledge, called "knowledge representation schemes" (e.g., Barr and Feigenbaum, 1981; Brachman and Levesque, 1985; Waterman, 1986), the purpose of this chapter is to determine the most suitable knowledge representation scheme for the project risk management system.

First, typical knowledge representation schemes are briefly overviewed. These include semantic networks, frames, production systems, and structured projection systems. Next, characteristics of these four knowledge representation schemes and project risk management domain are analyzed to identify a method that is suitable to represent the domain knowledge. Finally, in Section 5.3, more detailed quantitative discussions about comparisons of these knowledge representation schemes are added, which will support the above decision. Therefore, those who do not have a special interest in the rather technical aspects of knowledge representation can skip Section 5.3.

5.1 OVERVIEW

This section reviews the three most common knowledge representation schemes: semantic networks, frames, and production systems, as well as structured production systems that are a special form of production systems. Those who are familiar with these knowledge representation schemes can skip this section.

5.1.1 Semantic Networks

Semantic networks, originally invented as psychological models of human memory (Quillian, 1975), are based on a network structure that consists of nodes connected by links. The nodes represent concepts or events. The links specify interrelationships between the nodes. For example, "IS-A" is a link that describes a generalization relation, like "Cat is a mammal," where cat and mammal are nodes. Another example, "HAS-PART," is used like "Mammal has hair," where mammal and hair are nodes. These two examples can be represented in semantic network form, as shown in Fig. 5.1. The semantic network segment can also indicate that, since cats are mammals, and since mammals have hair, then cats have hair, even though the last statement (i.e., cats have hair) was not explicitly stated. Relevant facts about an object or concept can be explicitly and succinctly inferred from the nodes to which they are linked, without searching through a large knowledge base (Barr and Feigenbaum, 1981).

5.1.2 Frames

Frames were originally proposed (Minsky, 1975) as a basis for understanding visual perception, natural-language dialogues, and other complex behaviors (Barr and Feigenbaum, 1981). Minsky (1975) explained frames as follows:

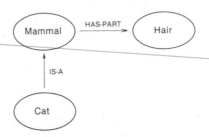

Figure 5.1. Semantic network.

When one encounters a new situation (or makes substantial changes in one's view of a problem), one selects from memory a structure called a *frame*. This is a remembered framework to be adapted to fit reality by changing details as necessary. A *frame* is a data-structure for representing a stereotyped situation like being in a certain living room or going to a child's birthday party. Attached to each frame are several kinds of information. Some of this information is about how to use the frame. Some is about what one can expect to happen next. Some is about what to do if these expectation are not confirmed.

A frame is a hierarchically organized network of nodes and relations, where the upper nodes represent general concepts or events, and the lower nodes represent more specific instances of those concepts or events. Each node is defined by a collection of attributes, called slots, and values of those slots. For example, simple frames for a table are shown in the following list.

Table Frame

AKO: Furniture

Shape: round or polygon

Number-of-legs: an integer (DEFAULT = 4)

Number-of-chairs:

range: an integer

if-needed: IF for-reading THEN one,

IF for-dining THEN more-than Number-of-family,

OTHERWISE 4.

Smith's-Table Frame

AKO: Table

Shape: quadrangle

Number-of-legs: 6

Number-of-chairs: -

The "AKO" (A-Kind-Of) slot is used to represent a generalization relation, much like the "IS-A" link in semantic networks. The content of the "range" slot in the "Table Frame" is an expectation about how many chairs the "Number-of-chairs" might have. The "if-needed" slot has procedures that can be used to determine the slot's value (i.e., "Number-of-chairs") if necessary. In the "Smith's-Table Frame," there is no value in the "Number-of-chairs" slot. However, it can be determined by the slot in the upper frame (i.e., the Table Frame).

5.1.3   Production Systems

Production systems were originally presented as models of human reasoning (Newell and Simon, 1972). Production systems consist of rules, called "production rules" or "productions," in the form of condition–action pairs such as "If this condition occurs, then do this action." For example,

If you need this article And its price is reasonable, Then you buy it.

Newell's idea was to represent long-term memory as production rules and short-term memory as a set of conditions. Each production rule indicates that if you recognize some conditions in short-term memory, then you take some actions. These actions may change the content of short-term memory, which will then evoke other production rules. A simple example is shown in Fig. 5.2. In long-term memory, there are three production rules. When you recognize condition R in short-term memory, the second production rule (if R then Q) in long-term memory is executed, and action Q is added

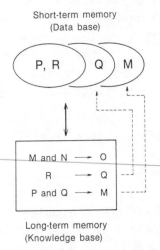

Figure 5.2. Production system.

to short-term memory as a new condition. That causes the third production rule (if P and Q then M) and, as a consequence, M is inferred and added to short-term memory. In AI or knowledge-engineering fields, long-term memory is sometimes called a "knowledge base" and short-term memory a "data base."

5.1.4 Structured Production Systems

Production systems have most often been used in AI programs to represent a body of knowledge (Barr and Feigenbaum, 1981). There are, however, some disadvantages, one of which is inefficiency of program execution and knowledge base maintenance. This is because production systems must perform *every production rule* in the knowledge base by match-action cycle during program execution, and also because engineers have to check *every production rule* to maintain (e.g., add, delete, or change) production rules in the knowledge base. One solution to this problem is to categorize the production rules into several knowledge sources. In this book this type of production system is called a "structured production system."

5.2 DETERMINATION OF KNOWLEDGE REPRESENTATION SCHEME

Determination of a suitable knowledge representation scheme is one of the most important steps in developing knowledge-based systems because it significantly affects efficient implementation and use of such systems. The purpose of this section is to select a knowledge representation scheme with characteristics that will fit those of the domain knowledge. In this section, the candidates for knowledge representation schemes are limited to the four typical schemes described in the previous section (i.e., semantic networks, frames, production systems, and structured production systems). This is because investigating other original schemes is beyond the scope of this book.

5.2.1 Classification of Knowledge Representation Schemes

The central issue in this section is how to classify the four knowledge representaion schemes so that one will be easily identified as s suitable scheme for representing domain knowledge. There has been no systematic method discovered until now (Niwa et al., 1984). Therefore, the method used will select a scheme in which declarative/procedural and uniform/structured axes were used. Since this method is primarily a rough qualitative analysis, quantitative analysis is presented Section 5.3 to support the result.

The first step is to clarify knowledge representation schemes in terms of their declarative and procedural characteristics. Although the dispute between declarative vs. procedural knowledge representation (Winograd, 1975) has been important in the historical development of AI techniques (Barr and Feigenbaum, 1981), very basic ideas of these characteristics are discussed in this section. Declarative representations express static aspects of concepts or events, and their relations, which are manipulated by another set of procedures. Therefore, as described in the previous section, semantic networks are declarative representations. Frames are basically declarative, although procedural mechanisms (often called "procedural attachments") such as "if-needed" are attached to them. Procedural representations incorporate both knowledge about static aspects of subjects and how to use this knowledge. Production systems (and also structured production systems) are primitive examples of procedural representations. Individual production rules of long-term memory are forced to interact through short-term memory as described in the previous section.

The next step is to classify the four knowledge representations in terms of uniform/structured characteristics. Semantic networks are uniform network structures consisting of nodes connected by links. Frames are structured knowledge representation schemes because each node is defined by attributes and their values. Production systems are also uniform; all productions are expressed in IF-THEN- form. Structured production systems are structured because productions are categorized into several knowledge sources.

The results of the above discussions are diagrammed in Fig. 5.3. The horizontal axis represents declarative or procedural classifications. The vertical axis represents uniform or structured classifications. Semantic networks are both declarative and uniform in their knowledge representation, whereas frames are declarative and structured. Production systems are procedural and uniform, and structured production systems are procedural and structured.

5.2.2 Classification of Domain Knowledge

Classify domain knowledge so that it will fall into one of the four areas defined by the declarative/procedural and uniform/structured axes in Fig.

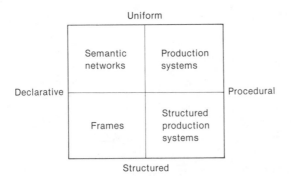

Figure 5.3. Rough classification of knowledge representation schemes.

5.3. One characteristic of domain knowledge is that it is more procedural than declarative. More specifically, risk knowledge represents such relationships as "risk factors cause risks" or "risks cause other risks if no risk-reducing strategies are used," as shown in the risk mechanism model in Section 4.1.

In terms of uniform or structured characteristics, domain knowledge is structured. This is because knowledge concerning risks is classified into risk factors or risks, as explained in Section 4.1. Risk factors are classified into three groups: contractual defects, managerial or operational errors, and environmental factors, as shown in Fig. 4.1. Risks themselves are related to the work packages in which the risks occur.

These discussions about classifications of both knowledge representation schemes and domain knowledge lead to the conclusion that structured production systems are suitable to project risk management systems. This is because characteristics of structured production systems and domain knowledge are both procedural and structured.

5.2.3 Determined Knowledge Representation Scheme

The risk mechanism model in Fig. 4.1 has been refined and obtained a domain knowledge structure, as shown in Fig. 5.4. Each risk factor has been divided into two stages (e.g., managerial or operational errors in the planning stage cause those in the execution stage, and so on). Work packages are explicitly shown in the figure to reflect the idea of the standard work package method described in Section 4.1 (i.e., risk knowledge from a certain project can be transferred to other projects by connecting the risks to work packages of projects).

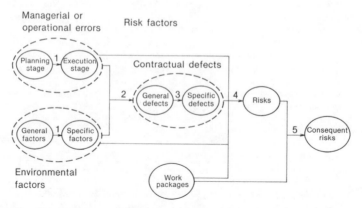

Figure 5.4. Domain knowledge structure. (From Niwa, et al. 1984. Reprinted with permission. © 1984 AAAI.)

Since every construction project has starting and ending points, the causal relationships in Fig. 5.4 flow in one direction (from left to right) along a time dimension. Consequently, knowledge can easily be described by such production rules as

- If (risk factors) Then (risk factors),
- If (risk factors) and (work packages) Then (risks), and
- If (risks) and (work packages) Then (risks).

The production rules are classified into five knowledge sources, according to the temporal order in Fig. 5.4. (The numbers in Fig. 5.4 correspond to the knowledge sources.) Sample production rules are as follows:

Rule 1001.

    If (carelessness in sales department)

    Then (noncompliance to standards by project managers), and
        (lack of coordination by project managers).

Rule 2001.

    If (complicated law), and
        (insufficient precautions by sales department)

    Then (contract defects in scope of equipment supply), and
        (contract defects in force major).

Rule 3001.

    If (contractual defects in scope of equipment supply)

Then (contractual defects in scope of site test), and
(contractual defects in limit of site entrance by inspector), and
(contractual defects in the supply of temporary facilities).

Rule 4001.

If (poor management control by project manager), and
(approval of hardware design)

Then (approval delay of instruction book in local language).

Rule 5001.

If (approval delay due to misunderstanding about amount of spare parts), and
(taking over the plant)

Then (owner rejects project).

Rule 1001 is an example of a production rule that deduces managerial/operational errors in the execution stage from those in the planning stage (see step 1 in Fig. 5.4), Rule 2001 is an example of a production rule that deduces contractual defects from managerial/operational errors and environmental factors (see step 2 in Fig. 5.4). Rule 3001 is an example of a production rule that deduces specific contractual defects from general contractual defects (see step 3 in Fig. 5.4). Rule 4001 is an example of a production rule that deduces risks from risk factors and project work packages (see step 4 in Fig. 5.4). Rule 5001 is an example of a production rule that deduces consequent risks from risks and project work packages (see step 5 in Fig. 5.4).

Every clause of the production rule is actually represented by a code in a computer to improve matching efficiency. The ASSOC function in LISP (e.g., Winston and Horn, 1981) combines the code with a translation when requested. Rule 1001, for example, is stored in the knowledge base as shown in the following example:

(rule 1001
(if (2b16))
(then (2a31) (2h31))).

5.3 EXPERIMENTAL COMPARISON*

This section discusses an experimental and quantitative comparison of knowledge representation schemes, and will reach the same conclusion as

*Some of the material in this section is derived from a previous paper (Niwa et al., 1984).

that of the previous section (i.e., structured production systems are appropriate for our purpose). Therefore, those who are not interested in rather technical AI discussions can skip this section. This section may be most interesting for those who have experience in developing knowledge bases because there are very few such comparison studies in spite of their importance (Niwa et al., 1984). This section may also be helpful for people who are interested in AI but who so far are not familiar with AI because it includes useful knowledge obtained through our experience that may not appear in other text books.

As described in the previous section, determining a knowledge representation scheme affects the efficient implementation and use of knowledge-based systems. It is for this reason that implementation difficulty and run-time efficiency in comparing knowledge representation schemes are discussed. However, this causes a problem when implementing knowledge-based systems that contain candidate knowledge representation schemes in order to compare such schemes and to select a suitable one from among them. A strategy for overcoming this problem is to implement "pilot" knowledge-based systems that have fundamental characteristics which may appear in "real" systems. Therefore, before this section read Section 6.1 in the next chapter in which fundamental functions of the "real" system (i.e., forward and backward reasoning) are described. However, those who are very familiar with forward and backward reasoning can proceed directly with this section.

5.3.1 Development of Experimental Pilot Systems

The knowledge representations discussed in this section are frames, production systems, and structured production systems, three out of the four representations in the previous section. This is because the characteristics of these three representations are at least either procedural or structured that are the domain's characteristics (See Fig. 5.3). Semantic networks, which have declarative and uniform characteristics, are omitted here.

All three pilot knowledge-based systems consist of knowledge bases and inference engines, and were developed on the VAX 11/780 computer using Franz-LISP. Three different types of knowledge base store the same knowledge. Although the details of their user interfaces (input/output, or system functions) will be described in the next chapter, the point emphasized in this section is that each user interface is exactly the same. The inference engines are capable of both forward and backward reasoning. In the forward reasoning mode, the systems are designed to warn the user (project manager) of risks that could follow from causes entered by the user. In the backward reasoning mode, the user enters a hypothetical risk, which the system confirms or denies as likely to occur according to the risk mechanism model.

A pilot system using frames, called a frame system, is implemented by a typical method (Winston and Horn, 1981) based on frame representation language (FRL). Three kinds of frames are made: "risk cause," "risk," and "work package." For example, risk frame 2103003 (consultant's approval delay) is shown in Fig. 5.5. This is a kind of (AKO) risk occurring at the hardware design approval stage. The risk factors are 2H31 (lack of project manager coordination) and 3Q01 (lack of customer or consultant ability). Its consequent risk is not recorded thus far. However, the frame indicates that risk 2103003 is a consequent risk of risk 2103007 (material upgrade for customer's future plan). This means that if no risk-reducing strategy is taken for risk 2103007, then risk 2103003 may occur. The frame for risk 2103003 is stored as

(2103003
    (AKO (VALUE (HARD-APPROVAL-RISK)))
    (NAME (VALUE (CONSULTANT'S APPROVAL DELAY)))
    (RISK-FACTOR (VALUE (2H31 3Q01)))
    (CONSEQUENT-RISK-FACTOR (VALUE (2103007))))).

As can be seen above, slots in the frame are used to represent risk causality (cause–effect relationships) as described above. AKO inheritance is used here, whereas procedural attachment is not employed. The inference engine

Risk 2103003	
AKO	Risks at hardware design approval stage
Name	Consultant's approval delay
Risk factors	Lack of project manager coordination (2H31), and
	Lack of customer or consultant ability (3Q01)
Consequent risks	
Consequent risk factors	Material upgrade request for customer's future plan (2103007)

Figure 5.5. Frame example. (From Niwa, et al. 1984. Reprinted with permission. © 1984 AAAI.)

of the pilot system is implemented by organizing basic frame-handling functions (Winston and Horn, 1981) so that forward and backward reasoning are performed.

A pilot system using production systems is called a production system. Its knowledge base is implemented using the production rules described in the previous section; however, here they are not divided into several knowledge sources. A core of forward and backward reasoning algorithms in the inference engine of the pilot production system is also implemented by applying a common method (Winston and Horn, 1981).

A pilot system using structured production systems is called a structured production system. Its knowledge base structure is exactly the same as described in the previous section; production rules are divided into five knowledge sources. A knowledge source control function is added to the pilot production system inference engine.

5.3.2 Implementation Difficulties

In general, decreasing implementation difficulty of one system element increases that of the other system elements. It is for this reason that we will discuss the implementation difficulty in knowledge bases and inference engines. "Difficulty" will be measured by the volumes of the knowledge base and inference engine; however, stress is also placed on developer's subjective judgments.

Knowledge Bases. The volume of the knowledge bases for the three pilot systems are:

Frame system	213 frames 29k characters
Production system	263 rules 15k characters
Structured production system	263 rules 15k characters

There are more characters in the frame system than in other systems because it was necessary in the frame system to replicate some related pieces of knowledge in different frames. The number of rules and characters for the production system and the structured production system are the same because both systems use the same rules, although the latter's rules were categorized. The number of frames, 213, is fewer than the number of production rules, 263, because some related rules were merged into a single frame.

Our results in evaluating the difficulty of implementing knowledge bases were derived from subjective judgments as well as from the volumes of the knowledge bases. The number of person-hours spent on the tasks was not used because as we became more experienced, each pilot system was developed in less time and more easily than the previous one.

- The production system knowledge base is easily implemented as far as the (If—Then—) pieces of knowledge are concerned. However, the domain structure shown in Fig. 5.4 cannot be represented explicitly.
- The structured production system knowledge base is easily implemented in representing pieces of knowledge and the domain structure. Each rule should be assigned to one of the five knowledge sources when the domain structure is represented.
- The frame system is rather difficult to implement because it is more structured than the other representations. It is necessary to determine what kinds of frames the system needs, what kinds of slots each frame needs, and how all the frames fit together into an AKO hierarchy. These items must be determined in such a way as to accurately represent the domain structure. The frames are found inadequate because local causal (cause–effect) relationships are more important than property inheritance in this domain (frames are suitable for representing property inheritance).

Inference Engine. The volumes of the inference engines for the three pilot systems are:

Frame system	14.3k characters
Production system	9.1k characters
Structured production system	9.5k characters

The fundamental algorithms for forward and backward reasoning in the inference engines of production systems are taken from a published source (Winston and Horn, 1981). However, some development is necessary to adapt such algorithms to the needs of the pilot systems. These developments are as follows, and also represent judgments of the implementation ease of the inference engines.

- The inference engine in the production system is the easiest to implement because little adaptation is necessary.

- The inference engine in the structured production system is also easy to implement. The algorithms for control knowledge sources are easily developed and incorporated into forward and backward algorithms.
- The inference engine in the frame system is rather difficult to implement. This is because it is necessary to develop forward and backward reasoning processes using FRL basic frame-handling functions.

5.3.3 Inference Run-Time Efficiency

As mentioned above, we must evaluate two pilot system aspects: ease of system implementation and use. These two aspects are often inversely related to each other. This subsection discusses the latter aspect and focuses on the inference run-time efficiencies of pilot systems.

CPU times for each pilot system were measured while running the same problems. The test contained both forward and backward reasoning. A sample of forward reasoning is when a user inputs Risk Factor Code 3O01 (lack of customer's English ability), Risk Factor Code 2E31 (project manager misguidance), and Work Package Code WT41.. (thermal plant civil work), and the system outputs Risk 41..005 (decrease in work efficiency due to poor utility) and Risk 41..010 (trouble with local labor due to different customs). The inference chain in the preceding case is shown in Fig. 5.6. A

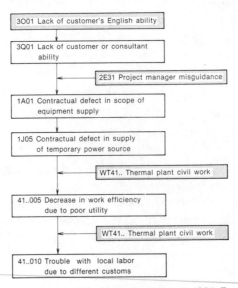

Figure 5.6. Inference chain example. (From Niwa, et al. 1984. Reprinted with permission. © 1984 AAAI.)

sample of backward reasoning starts from the bottom of the chain as a hypothesis. CPU time was measured by the Franz-LISP function PTIME (process time minus garbage-collection time). The measured inference time does not include user input or program output.

Experimental results for forward and backward reasoning are shown in Fig. 5.7. The sizes of the knowledge bases are varied as a parameter; three kinds of knowledge bases are adjusted to represent the same knowledge contents at any three knowledge volumes. [The number of Horn clauses was taken as a standard (Niwa et al., 1984).] The measured points in Fig. 5.7 are the average of three different problems, one of which is mentioned above. The results show that, for all knowledge base volumes, the frame system uses the least inference time, while the structured production system uses more, and the production system uses the most. As the amount of knowledge increases, the inference times of the frame system and the structured production system remain roughly constant; however, the inference time of the production system increases markedly. These results are due to the following factors:

- In the frame system, related pieces of knowledge are connected to one another, thereby limiting searches. This means that inference time is short and relatively insensitive to the size of the knowledge base.

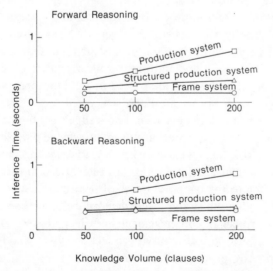

Figure 5.7. Experimental results of runtime efficiency.

- The number of rules to be searched in the structured production system is limited compared to that of the production system, which again means that inference time is short and is not strongly dependent on the size of the knowledge base.
- In the production system, the effect of increasing the knowledge volume is significant because all knowledge must be searched.

5.3.4 Results

We can summarize the previous discussion about the experimental comparison of pilot systems as follows:

- It is easy to implement both the knowledge base and the inference engine of the structured production system.
- Run-time efficiency of the structured production system is reasonable.

Therefore, the structured production system is appropriate for project risk management. This conclusion coincides with the result in Section 5.2.

5.4 SUMMARY

This chapter discussed knowledge representation of knowledge bases for project risk management. Four typical knowledge representation schemes—semantic networks, frames, production systems, and structured production systems—were briefly overviewed. They were then characterized in terms of their declarative/procedural and uniform/structured dimensions. Semantic networks are declarative and uniform, while frames are declarative and structured. Production systems are procedural and uniform, and structured production systems are procedural and structured.

Characteristics of risk management knowledge were then analyzed. Risk management knowledge is procedural; the knowledge represents causal relationships (i.e., risk factors cause risk, etc.). Risk management knowledge is also structured; causal relationships are categorized into five knowledge sources according to the temporal order of project activities.

Structured production systems were determined to be the knowledge representation of project risk management knowledge bases. This is because the characteristics of both structured production systems and risk management knowledge are procedural and structured.

Samples were given for five categories of production rules, which correspond to five knowledge sources. One rule deduces managerial/operational errors in the execution stage from those in the planning stage. The second rule deduces contractual defects from managerial/operational errors and environmental factors. The third rule deduces specific contractual defects from general contractual defects. The fourth rule deduces risks from risk factors and project work packages. The fifth rule deduces consequent risks from risks and project work packages.

In addition, an experimental comparison was presented to compare the ease of implementing the knowledge base and inference engine (forward and backward reasoning), as well as to compare run-time efficiencies. The results also showed the advantages of structured production systems for project risk management.

REFERENCES

Barr, A., and E. A. Feigenbaum, *The Handbook of Artificial Intelligence,* Vol. 1, William Kaufmann, Los Altos, CA, 1981.

Brachman, R. J., and H. J. Levesque (eds.), *Readings in Knowledge Representation,* Morgan Kaufmann, Los Altos, CA, 1985.

Minsky, M., "A framework for representing knowledge," In P. Winston (ed.), *The Psychology of Computer Vision,* McGraw-Hill, New York, 1975.

Newell, A., and H. A. Simon, *Human Problem Solving,* Prentice-Hall, Englewood, NJ, 1972.

Niwa, K., K. Sasaki, and H. Ihara, "An experimental comparison of knowledge representation schemes," *AI Magazine,* 5(2), p. 29, 1984.

Quillian, M. R., "Semantic Memory," In M. Minsky (ed.), *Semantic Information Processing,* MIT Press, Cambridge, MA, 1975.

Waterman, D. A., *A Guide To Expert Systems,* Addison-Wesley, Reading, MA, 1986.

Winograd, T., "Frame representations and the declarative/procedural controversy," In D. G. Bobrow and A. Collins (eds.), *Representation and Understanding,* Academic Press, New York, 1975.

Winston, P. H., and B. K. P. Horn, *Lisp,* Addison-Wesley, Reading, MA, 1981.

SUGGESTIONS FOR DISCUSSION

1. Select a domain with which you are familiar and identify the domain specialists' knowledge. Illustrate how it is represented by the following knowledge representation schemes:

- Semantic networks
- Frames
- Production system, and
- Structured production system

2. There are many reasons for structuring knowledge, of which the most common is high run-time efficiency. Explain why run-time efficiency of structured knowledge representation schemes is generally high.

3. It has been suggested that the reason project risk causality can easily be described by production rules is that projects have starting and ending points. Explain.

_____6
KNOWLEDGE UTILIZATION

This chapter discusses how we effectively use the knowledge in the knowledge base that was implemented in Chapter 5. The objective of this knowledge utilization is to help project managers control project risks by providing risk alarms. Inference methods, which are common expert system (knowledge-engineering) techniques, are initially used to facilitate the risk management. These methods will be useful when project managers check for potential risks.

However, as project managers become accustomed to these inference methods, they will no longer be satisfied with them. This is because they will feel that the answers provided by using such methods are too limited, although they know that there may be other knowledge in the knowledge base that can be used for solving their problems. Therefore, new methods to overcome such complaints must be developed.

6.1 INFERENCE METHODS

Inference is one of the three features that characterize expert systems, as described in Chapter 3. This section discusses how inference methods are successfully applied to project risk management. The shortcomings of inference methods as well as our strategy to overcome them is discussed in the following sections.

The basic idea of inference is briefly reviewed using production systems.* A simple example of inference is: "Both (A) and (If A Then B) deduce (B)." Another example is: "Altogether (A), (If A Then B), and (If B Then C) deduce (C)." The next example is: "Altogether (A), (If A Then B), (If B Then C), and (If C Then D) deduce (D)." As these examples show, the advantage of the inference method, when it is implemented in a computer, is easily understood. Pieces of knowledge (e.g., If A Then B) can be connected to one another automatically, even if they are separately placed in a knowledge base. This is particularly useful since people may overlook pieces of knowledge that should be connected.

"Forward reasoning" (sometimes called "forward chaining") and "backward reasoning" (sometimes called "backward chaining") are the most basic inference methods (e.g., Barr and Feigenbaum, 1981). Most other methods can be developed by combining these two methods. Therefore, forward and backward reasoning will be applied to project risk management.

Recently, a variety of expert system tools have been developed for building expert systems (e.g., Gevarter, 1987; Harmon et al., 1988; Waterman, 1986). It has been assumed that it is not necessary to know technical items such as forward and backward reasoning in order to use these tools. However, these tools will not be used. Rather basic inference methods will be applied for the following reasons.

- Mastering basic inference methods improves understanding and use of AI.
- Mastering such methods is not a difficult task because excellent textbooks are available (e.g., Winston and Horn, 1981). Sometimes mastering expert system tools is a rather tough task.
- Adding new original functions, if necessary, is more easily performed when using basic methods (e.g., LISP) than when using black-box tools. Actually, we will combine our new functions with these basic methods in Chapter 7.
- Mastering basic inference methods is one of the requirements neces-

*A brief explanation of production systems was presented in Section 5.1.

sary in evaluating and choosing appropriate tools from among many tools.

6.1.1 Forward Reasoning

Forward reasoning is an inference method that recursively concludes "Then part" of rules when "If part" of rules are given. For example, when (A) is given to a knowledge base consisting of (If A Then B), (If B Then C)', and (If C Then D), the result of forward reasoning is (B, C, and D).

Knowledge for project risk management was represented in production rules in Chapter 5. Risk causality was represented in the form of

- If (risk factors) Then (risk factors),
- If (risk factors) and (work packages*) Then (risks), or
- If (risks) and (work packages) Then (risks).

Therefore, forward reasoning is easily applied to project risk management in such a way as to determine risks when risk factors and work packages are given.

A forward reasoning example in the project risk management domain is shown in Fig. 6.1 (Niwa et al., 1984). The core of the forward reasoning program is written in LISP by using one of the most common algorithms (Winston and Horn, 1981). The first forward reasoning step is for the user (e.g., project manager) to input risk factors. The user can choose one of two ways of inputting risk factors: the menu method or the keyword-in-context (KWIC) method. The menu shows all the risk factors to the user so that he/she can select appropriate ones. This menu appears when the user inputs "?" after the first request from the computer, as shown in Fig. 6.1. In KWIC, the user first inputs character strings (e.g., words, phrases, or clauses). Risk factors containing these strings are then output. The top part of Fig. 6.1 demonstrates the KWIC method for inputting risk factors. The user has input two words and one phrase: "customer," "law," and "project manager." Then eight risk factors appear that have at least one of the three input strings. The user then specifies 3K01 (complicated laws), 3Q03 (custom differences between customer and consultant), and 2G31 (lack of examination by project managers).

---

*Definition of work package was presented in Section 4.1.

∗Please key-in strings for risk factors or "?"
> customer, law, project manager

∗Please specify risk factor codes
1G05 Contractual defect in customer's requirement time for approval
3O01 Lack of English ability of customer
3Q01 Lack of ability of customer or consultant
3Q03 Custom differences between customer and consultant
3K01 Complicated laws
3K02 Change in law or regulations
2E31 Project manager's misguidance
2G31 Lack of examination by project managers
> 3K01, 3Q03, 2G31

∗Please specify work package codes or "all'
> all

∗∗∗Risk Alarm∗∗∗
2103002 Approval delay due to misunderstanding about amount of spare parts
2103011 Civil approval delay due to differences in loading data between civil and
equipment subcontractors
5103013 Change of pipe foundation for very large equipment carry-in
6105001 Misunderstanding about amount of spare parts
6105011 Spare parts air cargo due to incomplete delivery

Figure 6.1. Forward reasoning example. (From Niwa, et al. 1984. Reprinted with permission. © 1984 AAAI.)

The next forward reasoning step is for the user to input word packages to be analyzed for possible risks. In Fig. 6.1, the user does not specify any particular work package but inputs "all." This means the user wants to know risks that may occur in all the work packages of the project.

Then, a list of risks appears, as shown in the bottom of Fig. 6.1. They are approval delay due to misunderstanding about amount of spare parts, civil approval delay due to differences in loading data between civil and equipment subcontractors, change of pipe foundation for very large equipment carry-in, misunderstanding about amount of spare parts, and spare parts air cargo due to incomplete delivery.

These forward reasoning processes are as follows. For example, the last two risks, such as risk (6105001) and risk (6105011), are deducted by using three rules (rules 1, 2, and 3) in the knowledge base, and two input risk factors (2G31) and (3Q03). Because "all" work packages have been specified, work packages that appear in the "If part" of these rules are satisfied.

Rule 1.

If (2G31: Lack of examination by project manager) and
(3Q03: Custom differences between customer and consultant)
Then (1A01: Contractual defects in scope of equipment supply)

Rule 2.

> If (1A01: Contractual defects in scope of equipment supply) and
> (WP6105: Work package of taking over)
>
> Then (6105001: Misunderstanding about amount of spare parts)

Rule 3.

> If (6105001: Misunderstanding about amount of spare parts) and
> (WP6105: Work package of taking over)
>
> Then (6105011: Spare part air cargo due to incomplete delivery)

Risk factors (3Q03), (2G31), and rule 1 deduce risk factor (1A01). Risk factor (1A01) and rule 2 deduce risk (6105001). Risk (6105001) and work package (WP6105) deduce risk (6105011).

In this example, no priorities are given to the output risks. Certainty factor (CF) was determined in medical consultation system, MYCIN (Shortliffe, 1976). However, we think it is desirable in management fields that all alternatives be shown to the user for evaluation and selection because such fields are too complex to rely entirely on a fully autonomous decision system.

6.1.2 Backward Reasoning

Backward reasoning is an inference method that proves a specified "Then part" of a rule (sometimes called a "hypothesis") by recursively confirming the existence of "If part" of rules. For example, if a knowledge base consists of (If A Then B) and (If B Then C), when a user wants to prove the occurrence of (C), he/she inputs (C) into the system. In other words, (C) is a hypothesis to be proven. The function of backward reasoning is, first, to find the If part of rules that conclude (C). In the previous example, the If parts that conclude (C) are (B) or (A). Therefore, the backward reasoning method asks the user, "Is there (B)?" or "Is there (A)?" If the user replies "Yes," the backward reasoning concludes and indicates, "Your hypothesis (C) may occur."

Thus, backward reasoning can easily be applied to project risk management in such a way as to check the possibility of occurrence of hypothesized risks that are input into the system. This is because the knowledge base for project risk management consists of risk causality rules such as: If (risk factors) Then (risk factors); If (risk factors) and (work packages) Then (risks); or If (risks) and (work packages) Then (risks). When the user inputs a risk as a hypothesis, the system asks about various conditions (e.g., risk factors and work packages), one after another, until the hypothesized risk is determined to be likely or not. The backward reasoning program is written in LISP by using one of the most common algorithms (Winston and Horn, 1981).

A backward reasoning example is shown in Fig. 6.2 (Niwa et al., 1984). The first step is for the user to specify a hypothesized risk. The KWIC method is also used in this step, as shown in the upper part of Fig. 6.2. A user has input "consultant" because he or she is concerned about risks relating to consultants. Then, he or she is informed of the risks from the knowledge base that include the string "consultant": consultant's approval

```
* Please key-in strings for risk
  > consultant

* Please specify risk codes
* 2103003 Consultant's approval delay
  41...030 Civil work delay due to insufficient negotiation with consultant
  51...051 Sudden material change due to consultant's error
  > 2103003

* Hypothesis 2103003
  Is this true: (2H31 Lack of project manager coordination)?
  > no
  Is this true: (3K01 Complicated laws)?
  > no
  Is this true: (3Q01 Lack in ability of the customer or consultant)?
  > yes
  Is this true: (2E31 Project manager misguidance)?
  > yes
  Is this true: (WP2103 Approval)?
  > yes

* Hypothesis 2103003 (Consultant approval delay) may occur
  Do you want to know how it is deduced?
  > yes

** The following rules were used * * *
Rule 3002 (If 2103007 and WP2103 then 2103003)
  * 2103007 Material upgrade request for customer's future plan
  * WP2103 Approval (yes input)
Rule 2002 (If 1A01 and WP2103 then 2103007)
  * 1A01 Contractual defects in scope of equipment supply
  * WP2103 Approval (yes input)
Rule 1003 (If 3Q01 and 2E31 then 1A01)
  * 3Q01 Lack in ability of customer and consultant (yes input)
  * 2E31 Project manager misguidance (yes input)
```

Figure 6.2. Backward reasoning example. (From Niwa, et al. 1984. Reprinted with permission. © 1984 AAAI.)

delay, civil work delay due to insufficient negotiation with consultant, and sudden material change due to consultant's error. Among these risks, the user selects the first risk (i.e., 2103003: "consultant's approval delay") as a hypothesis. This risk is the one (or very similar to the one) that the user is concerned about. The user wants to know its occurrence possibility.

The preceding procedure was designed for the following two reasons: most risks recur, as described in Section 2.2; and it is often difficult for users to express their concerns in a full sentence. Although this procedure is unique, in the project risk management domain users are comfortable with hypotheses expressed as character strings that include words, phrases, and clauses.

The next step, which appears in Fig. 6.2, consists of several questions and answers. These correspond to the inference processes of backward reasoning, which recursively confirms the existence of the If part of rules to prove the specified Then part as a hypothesis. The first question from the system, "Is this true: (2H31: Lack of project manager coordination)?," means "Is there a lack of project manager coordination in your project?" The user's reply, "no," means "No, I don't think so." The next question is, "Are there complicated laws in the customer's country?" The user inputs "no." The third question is, "Is there a lack in ability of the customer or consultant?" This time the user replies "yes" because he/she has been concerned about the consultant's ability. The next question is, "Is there project manager misguidance of the customer?" The answer "yes" is input. The final question is, "Is the work package that you want to analyze an approval?" The user replies "yes." Using these answers, the system provides a conclusion from backward reasoning, which is "Your hypothesis (i.e., consultant approval delay) may occur."

The final backward reasoning step is an explanation of the reasoning processes. Just after providing the conclusion, the system asks if the user wants to know how the conclusion was deduced, as shown in Fig. 6.2. The user replies "yes" to this question. The explanation is designed to demonstrate how rules are used to attain the conclusion (i.e., risk 2103003). The first rule is rule 3002: If (risk 2103007) and (work package WP2103), Then (risk 2103003). This rule was used to deduce hypothesized risk 2103003. One element of the If part of this rule is work package WP2103, which was input as "yes" by the user. The other element is risk 2103007, which in turn should be confirmed. The next rule 2002 deduced risk 2103007. The one element of the If part of rule 2002 that should be confirmed is risk factor 1A01, which was deduced by the third rule, rule 1003: If (risk factor 3Q01) and (risk factor 2E31), Then (risk factor 1A01). The two elements of the If part of this rule were input as "yes" by the user. The structure of the above explanation is shown in Fig. 6.3, where risk causalities are represented by nodes and arrows. For example, the three nodes in the top of the figure mean that "If WP2103 and 2103007, then 2103003." The shadowed nodes correspond to the items that the user entered as "yes." Therefore, the top node, risk 2103003, occurs.

6.1.3 Advantages of Inference Methods

From our experience, forward and backward reasoning, which are the most typical expert system techniques, are very useful for project risk management. Project managers can use forward reasoning to determine possible risks when they notice risk factors such as difficult economic/political conditions in a client's country, severe environmental factors, or contractual defects.

Project managers can use backward reasoning to confirm the occurrence of risks in many cases. For example, top management may often (and suddenly) ask project managers whether some specific risks may occur in their projects. Another example is when project managers want to know the occurrence possibility of risks that happened during other projects in the same client's country or with the same subcontractors.

The explanation function of backward reasoning is also very useful. Many questions from the system during the explanation process help project managers identify risk factors that are involved.

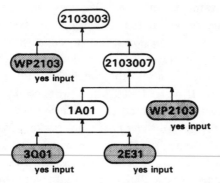

Figure 6.3. Structure of explanation in backward reasoning example

6.2 BEYOND INFERENCE: NEED FOR ASSOCIATION

6.2.1 Expert System Inference Methods vs. Actual Human Knowledge Association

Project managers have used an expert system that consists of forward and backward reasoning with considerable satisfaction. However, as they become accustomed to this system, they begin to find that the system answers are too limited. They know that, in the knowledge base, there are many more pieces of knowledge that should be output in addition to those actually provided. They know this because *they* provided knowledge obtained from their experience and *they* checked the knowledge before inputting it into the knowledge base, as described in Section 4.2.

A very simple example of this situation is shown in Figure 6.4. There are four production rules in the knowledge base. These rules were previously provided by the user. They are:

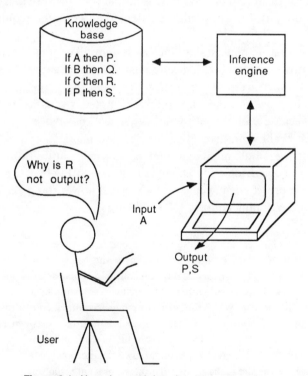

Figure 6.4. Users' complaint about expert systems.

1. If A Then P.
2. If B Then Q.
3. If C Then R.
4. If P Then S.

When the user wants to know the consequence of A, he inputs A into the system; then forward reasoning in the inference engine outputs P (by using production rule 1) and S (by combining production rules 1 and 4). However, the user feels that the answer is too limited because he/she knows that R exists in the knowledge base and because he/she thinks that R should be output in this situation. The most plausible solution to this problem is that project managers should have determined more relations among the pieces of knowledge, such as more production rules (e.g., If A Then R, of If P Then R for the preceding example) when the knowledge base was implemented. However, the project managers' response to this was that it was impossible for them to make more rules at that time because they could not foresee all the possible knowledge relations that would be required in the future.

Project managers understand that this system, like other expert systems, is limited to the extent of its logically related knowledge, the fundamental relations of which were determined at the time the knowledge base was implemented. However, they are still not completely satisfied with this explanation because *they* can easily perform such knowledge utilization that they requested above in their everyday decision making.

Let us then examine an actual human knowledge utilization. An actual human knowledge association example is shown in Fig. 6.5. This was observed during project management of a thermal power station construction project in a developing country (Niwa, 1986):

The project manager had accumulated a great deal of risk experience, such as equipment re-orders due to oversights involving foreign standards, design changes due to owner's incorrect data on soil, additional designs due to lack of interlocking devices with other subsystems, and requests for assembling spare parts at the site. When the project manager is informed of Situation 1, "civil approval delay due to differences in loading data between civil and equipment subcontractors," by telex from his site, his mind is stimulated to recall Situation 2, "design changes due to owner's incorrect data on soil." He therefore gives the site manager instructions to prevent Situation 2. This is the type of intuition that is focused on here, and is called *knowledge association*.

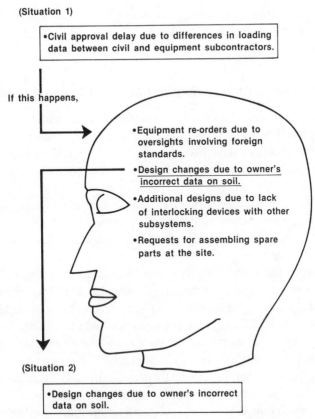

(Situation 1)

•Civil approval delay due to differences in loading data between civil and equipment subcontractors.

If this happens,

•Equipment re-orders due to oversights involving foreign standards.

•Design changes due to owner's incorrect data on soil.

•Additional designs due to lack of interlocking devices with other subsystems.

•Requests for assembling spare parts at the site.

(Situation 2)

•Design changes due to owner's incorrect data on soil.

This should be taken care of.

Figure 6.5. Human knowledge association example.

Knowledge association is defined as the process whereby the absorption of one piece of knowledge, i.e., Situation 1, stimulates the mind and causes it to recall another piece of knowledge, Situation 2. Other actual examples are: If Situation 1 is "price hikes due to ordering delays," then Situation 2 is "additional payments to local labor due to inappropriate escalation clauses."; and If Situation 1 is "material changes due to antipollution regulations," then Situation 2 is "wage hikes due to revisions in local labor laws."

This observation coincides with that of many other studies (Dreyfus and Dreyfus, 1980; Dreyfus, 1981; Dreyfus and Dreyfus, 1986; Kahneman et al., 1982; Klein, 1980; Morris, 1967; Silverman, 1985), which reported that human experts, unlike expert systems, do not always reason in terms of logical sets of knowledge. Rather, in their everyday decision-making and management processes, they intuitively utilize their knowledge, which is based on concrete experience.

6.2.2 Knowledge Association for Improving Expert Systems

This project managers' request is a situation in which managers want to be informed of knowledge from the knowledge base in regard to different contexts that could not have been expected at the time the knowledge base was implemented. In other words, they want expert systems to perform the function of *knowledge association*. This is a very difficult problem for existing expert systems because their inference mechanisms logically draw new conditions from given facts, as described in Section 3.1. Thus, their answers are only derived from the set of initial knowledge and the knowledge obtained by inference.

In regard to this limitation, there are three different viewpoints (Niwa, 1988b). The first is to say that this process should not be required of expert systems because such systems are too naive to accomplish knowledge association. In other words, knowledge engineering should be regarded as an efficient programming style that permits highly modular knowledge representation. This is most applicable to "rigid domains," such as plant control and process control domains, that logically use scientifically established knowledge rather than specialists' knowledge obtained through experience.

Another viewpoint is that, for successful application of expert systems, we should turn our attention away from ill-structured management domains to domains in which structure and function are well defined. By logically representing the domain's structure and function, a domain model can be constructed. Such a model is sometimes called "deep knowledge," whereas domain specialists' knowledge obtained through experience is sometimes called "shallow knowledge" (Hart, 1982; Michie, 1982). The deep knowledge is incorporated into the system so that it can be used for problem solving. The diagnosis of digital circuits is a typical example of such a well-structured domain (Davis et al., 1982).

The third viewpoint is to overcome the above problem. If the problem is solved, expert systems will become more useful even for solving problems in ill-structured domains.

This book supports the third viewpoint. The world is advancing into a post-industrial society, which may also be called an information-intensive society. In such a society, domain specialists' knowledge obtained through experience will become a valuable competitive resource, whereas scientific knowledge or knowledge appearing in standard textbooks will be easily accessible through information networks and various data bases. Therefore, the need for knowledge-based systems that handle domain specialists' knowledge will become greater than ever in many fields. The previous situation in project risk management is one of the earliest examples that will certainly appear in many fields in the very near future.

6.3 KNOWLEDGE ASSOCIATION METHOD

6.3.1 Related Research

We will briefly review two existing areas of research, which will affect our approach to knowledge association. These involve a synonym dictionary in the information retrieval field and analogical reasoning in the AI field. These two methods are considered because they seem to be closely related to knowledge association. However, as described below, these methods cannot accomplish knowledge association.

Information retrieval (IR) is one of the established disciplines in computer technology (e.g., Salton, 1968). A synonym dictionary or thesaurus in IR is used for retrieval of associated words, such as "fun" and "amusement," or "white" and "nurse." This is possible because similar or related words were organized in the form of a dictionary and stored in a computer in advance. However, this retrieval method cannot be applied to knowledge association because knowledge is expressed not in words but in clauses, phrases, or sentences.

Analogical reasoning is an area of recent research in AI for investigating human intuitive processes (Carbonell, 1984). Analogical reasoning uses past experience by focusing on the similarities between new and past situations. The main difficulties in applying analogical reasoning to knowledge association involve two factors: (1) there are various similarities that depend on purposes and circumstances that cannot easily be foreseen; and (2) there are other relevant factors, in addition to similarity, between new and past situations.

6.3.2 The Method

From the previous discussions we can identify two problems with knowledge association:

- Knowledge association does not occur between *words*, but between situations that are represented in sentences.
- Relationships between such situations cannot generally be determined *in advance*, but can only be determined when it is necessary to use knowledge association.

Regarding the first problem, we will develop a method in which " word" operations can be explicitly included because such operations are very efficient. We will decompose the knowledge association process (from situation 1 to situation 2) so that words can explicitly appear. The most simple method is to insert a "keyword" between two situations (situation 1 and situation 2). The whole process is divided into two processes: process 1 and process 2, which is shown as a "knowledge association process model" in Fig. 6.6. In the first step of our research, the KWIC method is applied to process 2 in such a way that the knowledge base may be searched to find situation 2 (or association knowledge), which has the keyword in its sentence. Although the new process is easier than the original process from a technical viewpoint, a new problem appears here in what the meaning of the keyword is from the viewpoint of knowledge association. The two processes of the new model can correspond to our view of knowledge association: If situation 1 happens, then other situations relating to "something" may happen. The idea is to represent this something in terms of a keyword.

However, a difficulty still remains in process 1. The decomposition of the association process (Fig. 6.6) does not seem to solve the second problem, such as many varieties of relationships may produce keywords (instead of situation 2 here) from situation 1, and we cannot determine such relationships in advance. Thus, we will explore a way in which such relationships may be determined just when they are required. How to do it? Today's computer cannot do this. Therefore, a tentative answer is that those who require knowledge association should do it. Thus, we propose that, in process 1, the user (human) provides keywords just when situation 1 is given.

Figure 6.6. Knowledge association process model. (From Niwa, 1986. Reprinted with permission.© 1986 IEEE.)

This function of providing keywords should be performed by human intuitive ability.

The advantages of this method based on the knowledge association model (Fig. 6.6) are that process 2 is easily implemented in computers, and that keyword input in process 2 is easily implemented, and the keyword interface is easy to use by humans. This knowledge association method also has advantages from the viewpoint of knowledge utilization. Nonrelated knowledge in the knowledge base (i.e., knowledge that could not be related to other knowledge at the time of the knowledge base implementation) can be extracted in connection with other knowledge by effectively using human intuitive (or association) ability.

This method may be especially effective for application to knowledge bases in management domains that consist of several parts corresponding to different organizations, as shown in Fig. 6.7. This is because, for such domains, it becomes more and more desirable to use as many pieces of knowledge as possible to solve today's complicated problems, even if they are not related to one another by inference chains when they were input into the knowledge base.

However, the method should be applied solely to moderately ill-structured (or semistructured) domains. In severely ill-structured domains, such as innovation processes, the method cannot be applied well because there is a lack of suitable prior experience with new situations.

The risk management of large construction projects is one of the most suitable fields for applying this method. Details of this application are described in Chapter 7.

6.4 SUMMARY

This chapter discussed knowledge utilization methods of knowledge in the knowledge base that was developed in Chapter 5. Two of the most typical inference methods—forward reasoning and backward reasoning—were applied and found very useful for project risk management. Since knowledge base was implemented using production rules that represented risk causality, good use could be made of forward reasoning in determining possible risks when risk symptoms were observed. Backward reasoning was also effectively used to confirm the occurrence possibilities of some specified risks.

However, as project managers became accustomed to this system, they

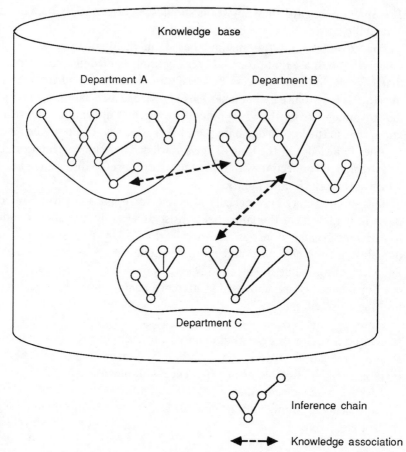

Figure 6.7. Knowledge base structure to which knowledge association method can be effectively applied.

began to find that the answers the system provided were too limited. Project manager knowledge association examples during actual project management were observed and knowledge association was defined as the process whereby the absorption of one piece of knowledge stimulates the mind, causing it to recall another piece of knowledge. Project managers wanted to be informed of knowledge from the knowledge base regarding different contexts that could not have been expected at the time the knowledge base was implemented. Current techniques such as expert systems, information retrieval, and analogical reasoning cannot accomplish this.

Two problems that make knowledge association difficult were identified:

- It is performed not between words but between situations (expressed in sentences).
- The relationships between such situations cannot be determined in advance.

Therefore, a method in which "word" operations can be explicitly included for the first problem was proposed which involved separating knowledge association process by "keywords." To overcome the second problem, these keywords are provided by the user by using intuitive ability when using the system. When keywords are given, the computer can use the KWIC (keyword in context) method to search its knowledge base and find knowledge that includes the keywords. This knowledge is "association knowledge."

In the following chapter, this method will be reinterpreted in the context of a new concept—the human–computer cooperative system. The application of this method to project risk management will also be described.

REFERENCES

Barr, A., and E. A. Feigenbaum, *The Handbook of Artificial Intelligence*, Vol. 1, William Kaufmann, Los Altos, CA, 1981.

Carbonell, J. G., "Learning by analogy: Formulating and generalizing plans from past experience," In R. S. Michalski, J. G. Carbonnell, and T. M. Mitchell (eds.), *Machine Learning—An Artificial Intelligence Approach,* Springer-Verlag, Berlin, 1984.

Davis, R., H. Shrobe, W. Hamscher, K. Wieckert, M. Shirley, and S. Polit, "Diagnosis based on structure and function," *Proc. of American Association for Artificial Intelligence National Conference*, p. 137, 1982.

Dreyfus, S. E., and H. L. Dreyfus, "A five stage model of the mental activities involved in directed skill acquisition," Report ORC 80-2, University of California at Berkeley, 1980.

Dreyfus, S. E., "Formal models vs. human situational understanding: Inherent limitations on the modeling of business expertise," Report ORC 81-3, University of California at Berkeley, 1981.

Dreyfus, H. L., and S. E. Dreyfus, *Mind Over Machine*, Free Press, New York, 1986.

Gevarter, W. B., "The nature and evaluation of commercial expert system building tools," *IEEE Computer*, **20**(5), p. 24, 1987.

Harmon, P., R. Maus, and W. Morrissey, *Expert Systems Tools and Applications*, John Wiley, New York, 1988.

Hart, P. E., "Direction for AI in the eighties," *SIGART*, **79**, p. 11, 1982.

Kahneman, D., P. Slovic, and A. Tversky (eds.), *Judgment Under Uncertainty: Heuristics and Biases*, Cambridge University Press, 1982.

Klein, G. K., "Automated aides for the proficient decision maker," *Proc. of IEEE International Conference on Cybernetics and Society*, p. 301, 1980.

Michie, D., "High-road and low-road programs," *AI Magazine*, **3**(1), p. 21, 1982.

Morris, W. T., "Intuition and relevance," *Management Science*, **14**, p. B157, 1967.

Niwa, K., K. Sasaki, and H. Ihara, "An experimental comparison of knowledge representation schemes," *AI Magazine*, **5**(2), p. 29, 1984.

Niwa, K., "Knowledge-based human–computer cooperative system for ill-structured management domains, *IEEE Transactions on Systems, Man, and Cybernetics*, **SMC-16**(3), p. 335, 1986.

Niwa, K., "Human–computer cooperative system: Conceptual basis, sample system evaluation, and R&D directions," *Proc. of American Society of Mechanical Engineers Manufacturing International*, p. 87, 1988b.

Salton, G., *Automatic Information Organization and Retrieval*, McGraw-Hill, New York, 1969.

Shortliffe, E. H., *Computer-Based Medical Consultations: MYCIN*, Elsevier, New York, 1976.

Silverman, B. G., "Expert intuition and ill-structured problem solving," *IEEE Transactions on Engineering Management*, **EM-32**(1), p. 29, 1985.

Waterman, D. A., *A Guide to Expert Systems*, Addison-Wesley, Reading, MA, 1986.

Winston, P. H., and B. K. P. Horn, *LISP*, Addison-Wesley, Reading, MA, 1981.

SUGGESTIONS FOR DISCUSSION

1. Select a domain with which you are familiar and give situations or problems in which:

   • Forward reasoning can be used, and
   • Backward reasoning can be used.

2. It has been suggested that the explanation function of backward reasoning of the project risk management system is useful to project managers. Explain this.

3.   Give examples in which humans may intuitively utilize their knowledge.

4.   Tell why it is difficult to treat knowledge association in project risk management domain by existing methods such as:

   - Inference
   - Information retrieval, and
   - Deep-knowledge (model) methods. (See Section 3.2.)

5.   Using Fig. 6.7, explain why knowledge association method proposed in this chapter can be effectively applied to knowledge bases that consist of several parts corresponding to different organizations.

6.   Give example fields in which knowledge bases consist of several parts corresponding to different organizations.

___7
HUMAN–COMPUTER COOPERATIVE SYSTEM

This chapter presents a new concept—a human–computer cooperative system—and integrates the discussions of previous chapters. Special interest here is how to integrate these elements into a total system. To explore this concept, the expected role of future computers is discussed.

A human–computer cooperative system for project risk management is developed. The system functions are designed according to the requirement analysis presented in Chapter 2. Knowledge is stored in the knowledge base by using a structured production system representation. knowledge utilization is applied by forward and backward reasoning, and by knowledge association methods.

Next, this chapter demonstrates examples of system usage. Finally, after describing users' positive and negative evaluations of the system, some potential application fields of the system are presented.

7.1 HUMAN–COMPUTER COOPERATION

7.1.1 Trends in Main Computer Roles

There are two different aspects in proposing a new system concept (i.e., a human–computer cooperative system). Project managers need to overcome the limitation of existing expert systems that are encountered during the development of a knowledge-based system for project risk management. This was described in Chapter 6. The other is a view of the trend of the main roles of computers in our society, which is discussed below. The relationship between these two aspects will also be described in this section.

Our view of the trends of the main role of computers is briefly summarized in Fig. 7.1. In the past, computers were mainly used for numerical calculations in physics, engineering, etc., as well as for data processing in accounting, statistics, etc. The role of computers in those days was to provide "computation support." Using stored programs, computers calculated data that people input, and produced solutions. Computers were very useful because of their highly accurate performances.

Today, although computers are still used for calculations or data bases, "knowledge support" has received particular attention largely because of the emergence of knowledge-based systems (expert systems). Expert systems store domain specialists' knowledge obtained through experience. Expert systems are especially useful to novices in accessing knowledge which has been provided by domain specialists (experts). The point about such expert systems is that, in addition to algorithms (program routines), human knowledge is incorporated into computer systems. Thus, computers are regarded as teachers or consultants of novices in many activities such as diagnosis, design, or monitoring.

In the future, computers will be used not only as teachers of novices, but as colleagues of experts. The expected function of computers is to stimulate or guide people's creative (or intuitive) thinking, in addition to performing the existing functions involving logical computing and knowledge bases.

	Past	Present	Future
Main role	Computation support	Knowledge support	Thinking support
Sample system	Computation system	Expert system	Human-computer cooperative system
Application fields	Calculations in • Physics • Engineering Data processing in • Accounting • Statistics	Guidance to novices in • Diagnosis • Design • Monitoring etc.	Cooperation with experts in • Engineering • Management • Marketing etc.

Figure 7.1. Trend of the main roles of computers.

The term *thinking support* is used in describing the future role of computers, as shown in Fig. 7.1. With the help of computers, people will be able to focus on intuitive thinking. Cooperation between humans and computers will result in better problem-solving ability. This relationship between humans and computers is called "human–computer cooperation," and the system that accomplishes this a "human–computer cooperative system."

7.1.2 Human-Computer Cooperative Approach to Knowledge Association

It seems too difficult for computers to perform knowledge association, which was defined as a process including situation 1 (initial knowledge) to situation 2 (association knowledge) in Section 6.2. On the contrary, humans do this every day with no particular difficulty. This problem seems very similar to that when knowledge engineering was first proposed (see Section 3.1). The problem then was that domain specialists could easily do what computers could not by using AI techniques. To overcome this problem, domain specialists' knowledge was newly introduced into computer systems as one of the subsystems (i.e., a knowledge base).

Human–computer cooperation is applied to knowledge association. To achieve human–computer cooperation in the knowledge association process, we must design a method in which humans and computers can perform their own roles (i.e., intuitive and logical roles, respectively), and in which computers stimulate or guide the human intuitive role. The first step in our research of this unexplored field is:

1. Computers should stimulate or guide human intuitive thinking.
2. Humans should intuitively provide "indication/hint" for knowledge association when situation 1 (initial knowledge) is given.
3. Computers should search the knowledge base to find situation 2 (association knowledge) by using the indication/hint that the human provided.

The point to be considered here is how to incorporate the human intuitive role into a more comprehensive computer system. As defined in Section 6.2, the knowledge association process starts from situation 1 (initial knowledge) and ends in situation 2 (association knowledge). The first idea is to separate the whole process into two parts; one of these will be performed by humans, which corresponds to item 2, and the other by computers, which corresponds to item 3. The next idea is to develop computer support functions that help humans perform their roles, which corresponds to item 1.

The heart of the first idea is shown in "human–computer cooperation in knowledge association," shown in Fig. 7.2. In this model, indicator/hint separates the process into two parts (i.e., process 1 and process 2). The structure of the "human–computer cooperation in knowledge association" (Fig. 7.2) completely coincides with the "knowledge association process model" (Fig. 6.6) presented in Section 6.2., if the indication/hint is substituted with a "keyword(s)." In Section 6.2 we developed the knowledge association process model in order to solve actual problems in project risk management, whereas the approach in this section is based on the consideration of a wider perspective of future roles of computers. Therefore, the coincidence of these two opposite (i.e., bottom up and top down) approaches indicates the soundness of the following idea:

> Humans perform process 1; when the human is informed of situation 1 (initial knowledge), then the human provides an indication/hint for knowledge association in terms of keywords by using human associative ability. The computer performs process 2; when the computer is informed of keywords, then the computer draws on its retrieval/pattern-matching ability to provide situation 2 (association knowledge).

With regard to the second idea, functions on the computer that help humans recall *keywords* as indicators/hints will be developed. The computer is designed to provide humans with suggestions that help them recall keywords when situation 1 (initial knowledge) is given. This function is called an "association guidance function." These suggestions should be appropriate to human characteristics, although this seems very difficult. How-

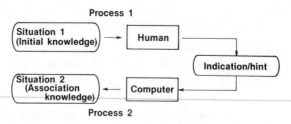

Figure 7.2. Human–computer cooperation in knowledge association.

ever, if the application fields and expected system users have been determined, appropriate sets of suggestions can be made. These are discussed in more detail in the next Section 7.1.3.

7.1.3 Human–Computer Cooperative System for Project Risk Management

The human–computer cooperative system for project risk management (Niwa, 1986, 1988b) consists of three subsystems: forward reasoning, backward reasoning, and knowledge association, as shown in Fig. 7.3. The first and second subsystems utilize existing expert system techniques, which were described in Section 6.1. The third subsystem is our newly proposed function that was described earlier in this chapter. The user can use a combination of these subsystems. For example, first the user is informed of risks (initial knowledge) through forward reasoning by inputting risk factors. Next he/she can obtain other possible risks (association knowledge) by human–computer cooperation. Finally, obtained risk (association risk) probability occurrences will be checked by backward reasoning.

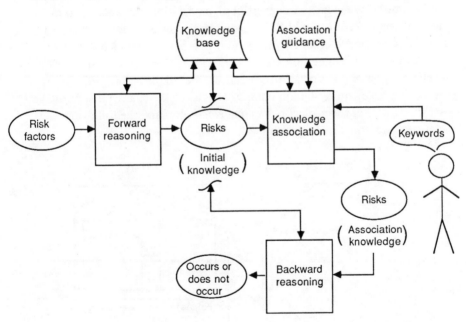

Figure 7.3. Structure of human–computer cooperative system for project risk management.

From the viewpoint of human–computer cooperation, the system can be considered to perform at two levels of cooperation, as shown in Fig. 7.4. The first level is performed with forward/backward reasoning subsystems and an knowledge association subsystem. The former two subsystems provide knowledge from the knowledge base using inference methods that are strictly logical. The latter subsystem provides nonlogically related knowledge from the knowledge base using human intuitive ability as its central function.

The second level is performed within the knowledge association subsystem so that this subsystem can provide nonrelated (or association) knowledge. Computer roles in the knowledge association subsystem are (1) to provide suggestions to stimulate or guide human intuition so that humans can recall keywords as indications/hints for association knowledge; (2) to search the knowledge base to find association knowledge by using the keywords. The human role in this subsystem is to recall (provide intuitively) keywords when initial knowledge is given.

One important function of the knowledge association subsystem is the computer function that provides humans with suggestions to help them recall keywords. We call these suggestions "association guidance." To make this function effective, apply "converting the point of view (of the user)." This "conversion" is effective for the user to recall keywords because it has been known to stimulate human thinking (Saeki, 1982; Murakami, 1985).

The suggestions (association guidance) should be appropriate to the characteristics of the system domain as well as to the characteristics of the user (human). For the project risk management domain, the following characteristics are taken into account:

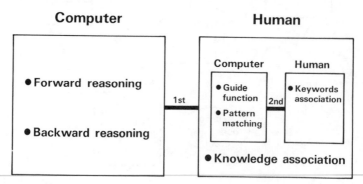

Figure 7.4 Two-level human–computer cooperation. 1st: the first level of cooperation; 2nd: the second level of cooperation.

- Position (executive, manager, or engineer),
- Purpose (planning, taking countermeasures, or risk finding), and
- Skill level (novice or expert).

According to the combination of these characteristics that the user specifies, the system is designed to provide different suggestions. Examples of these suggestions are demonstrated in the following section.

The use of association guidance to convert the user's point of view and the keyword pattern matching by the computer are diagrammed in Fig. 7.5. When a user wants to obtain association knowledge (situation 2) from initial knowledge (situation 1), he first specifies his characteristics (e.g., executive for position, planning for purpose, novice for skill-level). Some appropriate suggestions appear on the display for the user to convert the point of view, which helps the user recall keywords. These keywords are entered in by the user. The keywords are matched to the knowledge base and, as a result, association knowledge is output. If necessary, a thesaurus is used before pattern matching to obtain a wider range of keywords, which will produce more variety of association knowledge. (A thesaurus can be used in this step because the input is words—not phrases, clauses, or sentences—and the output is also words.) The obtained association knowledge (situation 2) can be stored for future use in the system as an association knowledge dictionary together with the initial knowledge (situation 1), the specified user characteristics, and the keywords.

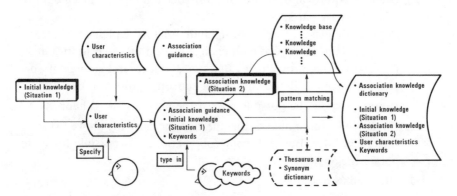

Figure 7.5. Knowledge association support mechanism. (From Niwa, 1986. Reprinted with permission. ©1986 IEEE.)

7.2 EXAMPLE OF SYSTEM USAGE

This section demonstrates an example of the human–computer cooperative system used in project risk management. The following is an easy-to-read personified dialogue between human and computer, where H means human (the user) and C means computer (Niwa, 1988b). This dialogue exactly corresponds to the actual input and output of the system (Figs. 7.6–7.11). The dialogue starts just after the user entered risk factors and work packages for forward reasoning, which are virtually the same procedures shown in Fig. 6.1. The first part of the dialogue (H1 and C1) shows how the forward reasoning subsystem warns the user (project manager) of risks (corresponding to the set of initial knowledge) that follow from causes entered by the user. The next part (from H2 to C9) demonstrates how the user is informed of other possible risks (corresponding to association knowledge) by the knowledge association subsystem (i.e., by using human associative ability guided by the computer). The final part of the dialogue (from H8 to H11) shows the association knowledge being checked by backward reasoning.

H1: I want to know the risks in the design approval phase from the following causes:
   –contractual scope defects in equipment supply,
   –misguidance of project manager,
   –lack in ability of customer or consultant.

C1: They are:
   (Risk 1) Approval delay due to misunderstanding about amount of spare parts,
   (Risk 2) Requests of material upgrade for future plan of owner,
   (Risk 3) Request of pipe path change from on-ground to in-trench,
   (Risk 4) Civil approval delay due to differences in loading data between civil and equipment subcontractors (see Fig. 7.6).

H2: I want to know the possible risks if the above (Risk 4) happens.

C2: I'm sorry I cannot answer the question, because the above list is all that I can infer. But with your cooperation, it is possible for us to obtain the answer.

H3: OK. Let's start.

C3: I would like to know more about you (see Fig. 7.7).
   What is your position: executive, manager, or engineer?

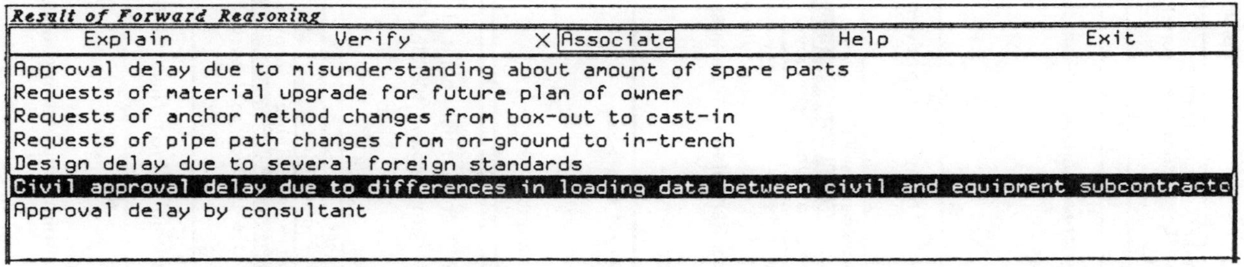

Result of Forward Reasoning

Explain	Verify	X Associate	Help	Exit

Approval delay due to misunderstanding about amount of spare parts
Requests of material upgrade for future plan of owner
Requests of anchor method changes from box-out to cast-in
Requests of pipe path changes from on-ground to in-trench
Design delay due to several foreign standards
Civil approval delay due to differences in loading data between civil and equipment subcontracto
Approval delay by consultant

Figure 7.6. Forward reasoning result example. (From Niwa, 1986. Reprinted with permission. ©1986 IEEE.)

```
┌──────────────────────────────────────────────────────────────┐
│      ▐Association Guidance▌              Keyword Underline      │
├──────────────────────────────────────────────────────────────┤
│ Position   : Executive  Manager  Engineer                      │
│ Purpose    : Plan (planning)  Do (countermeasure)  See (risk finding) │
│ Skill level: Novice  Expert                                    │
├──────────────────────────────────────────────────────────────┤
│ Do it ☐                                                        │
└──────────────────────────────────────────────────────────────┘
```

Figure 7.7. Specifications of user characteristics. (From Niwa, 1986. Reprinted with permission. ©1986 IEEE.)

```
┌──────────────────────────────────────────────────────────────┐
│ From the point of view of determining and preventing recurrence of │
│ technical trouble                                              │
│                                                                │
│ Your participants/elements concerned are:                      │
│  Machine eng.  Electric eng.  ▐Civil-works eng.▌               │
│ Click the one which is the source of your concern.             │
└──────────────────────────────────────────────────────────────┘
```

Figure 7.8. Association guidance 1: focus on matter of concern, and show participants/elements. (From Niwa, 1986. Reprinted with permission. ©1986 IEEE.)

```
┌──────────────────────────────────────────────────────────────┐
│ Put yourself in Civil-works eng.'s place.                      │
│                                                                │
│  What do you think causes the trouble ?                        │
│   soil                                                         │
│  What do you claim from the contractor ?                       │
│   re-test█                                                     │
└──────────────────────────────────────────────────────────────┘
```

Figure 7.9. Association guidance 2: convert user point of view, and keyword input. (From Niwa, 1986. Reprinted with permission. ©1986 IEEE.)

```
┌──────────────────────────────────────────────────────────────┐
│ Result of Association (Association Guidance)                   │
├──────────────────────────────────────────────────────────────┤
│    X │Verify│          Next Risk              Exit             │
├──────────────────────────────────────────────────────────────┤
│ Re-test of material due to poor interpretation by inspection company │
│ ▐Design changes due to owner's incorrect data on soil▌        │
│ Changes of construction equipment due to poor soil survey      │
└──────────────────────────────────────────────────────────────┘
```

Figure 7.10. Association result example. (From Niwa, 1986. Reprinted with permission. ©1986 IEEE.)

What is your purpose: planning, taking countermeasures, or risk finding?

Are you a: novice or expert?

H4: I am an engineer, my purpose is risk finding, and I am an expert.

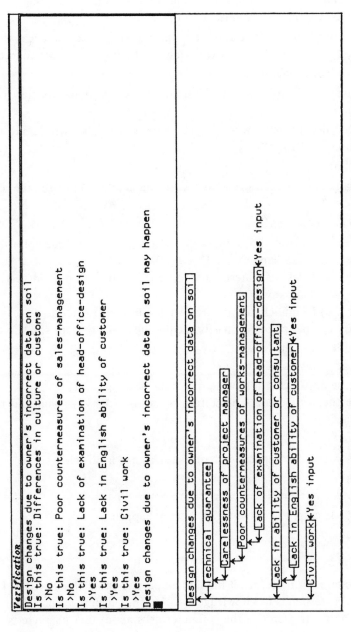

Figure 7.11. Backward reasoning result example. (From Niwa, 1986. Reprinted with permission. ©1986 IEEE.)

105

C4: In your case, we should focus our attention on "preventing recurrence of technical trouble" (see Fig. 7.8).

C5: The participants concerned are: machine engineer, electrical engineer, or civil works engineer. Which is the source of your concern?

H5: Civil works engineer.

C6: I suggest that you put yourself in the civil work engineer's place (see Fig. 7.9).

C7: What do you (civil work engineer) think, using keywords, are the causes of (Risk 4)?

H6: I think "soil."

C8: Thank you. What do you (civil work engineer) request from the contractor?

H7: I request "retest."

C9: Then my answer is: If the above (Risk 4) happens, the following risks may also happen (see Fig. 7.10).
(Risk a) Retest of material due to poor interpretation by inspection company.
(Risk b) Design change due to owner's incorrect soil data.
(Risk c) Change of construction equipment due to poor soil survey.

H8: Thank you. But I want to verify if the above (Risk b) will really occur in my case.

C10: Please answer the following questions (see Fig. 7.11).
Are there differences of culture or customs between you and the owner?

H9: No.

C11: Are your sales department countermeasures insufficient?

H10: No.
—More questions and answers are omitted here.—

C12: In your case, the above (Risk b) may happen.

H11: Thank you.

Let's examine in more detail the middle part of the dialogue (from H2 to C9) that corresponds to knowledge association, which is of special interest in this book. In step C3, the computer asks about user characteristics by showing the candidates that were previously made for the project risk management domain. The user specifies characteristics in step H4, which will be used to present appropriate guidance. Suggestion C4 helps the user focus his attention on the matter of concern (i.e., "preventing recurrence of technical trouble"), which corresponds to the characteristics that were entered in H4. The next guidance step, C5, shows the participants concerned. The user specifies the participant that is the cause of concern according to the guidance of the computer (H5). Then, the suggestion appears (C6) to convert the user's position to that previously specified. The questions of the computer, C7 and C8, are intended to stimulate or guide user association. The keywords, "soil" and "retest," are recalled intuitively by the user. They are then entered into the computer, as shown in H6 and H7. Next, these keywords are pattern-matched to the knowledge base to find risks (association knowledge) that involve at least one of the keywords (C9). The obtained association knowledge can be stored in the system, if the user wants, for future use as an association knowledge dictionary, together with the keywords and user characteristics.

The previous procedure (from H2 to C9) may be considered as determining or acquiring the following knowledge association (or rule):

If

[(Risk 4) Approval delay due to differences in loading data between civil and equipment subcontractors] happens,

Then you should take care of

[(Risk b) Design change due to owner's incorrect soil data].

It may be natural to think that this rule should have been determined in the knowledge base implementation phase and stored in advance. However, that could not be done during system development because it was difficult for knowledge suppliers to connect these two situations at the time of the knowledge base implementation. Generally speaking, in ill-structured or large-scale domains, it is very difficult to determine all the possible knowledge relationships at the time the knowledge base is implemented because all future possible situations cannot be foreseen.

The processes of association guidance for "manager" and "executive" are shown in Figs. 7.12 and 7.13. In the manager's case (Fig. 7.12), the first suggestion is for the user to focus on "finding and preventing trouble, as well as avoiding and transferring risks." The next is to show the manager's participants. These are company, client, consultant, consortium member, subcontractor, sales, and factory. In the same way, the first suggestion for

```
┌─────────────────────────────────────────────────────────────────┐
│     Association Guidance              Keyword Underline            │
├─────────────────────────────────────────────────────────────────┤
│ Position     : Executive   Manager   Engineer                     │
│ Purpose      : Plan (planning)  Do (countermeasure)  See (risk finding) │
│ Skill level  : Novice   Expert                                    │
├─────────────────────────────────────────────────────────────────┤
│ Do it ☐                                                           │
├─────────────────────────────────────────────────────────────────┤
│ Civil approval delay due to differences in loading data between civil and │
│ equipment subcontractors                                          │
│                                                                   │
│ From the point of view of finding and preventing trouble, and to  │
│ avoid or transfer risks                                           │
│                                                                   │
│ Your participants/elements concerned are:                         │
│  Company   Client   Consultant   Consortium member   Sub-contractor │
│  Sales    Factory                                                 │
│ Click the one which is the source of your concern.                │
└─────────────────────────────────────────────────────────────────┘
```

Figure 7.12. Association guidance for managers.

```
┌─────────────────────────────────────────────────────────────────┐
│     Association Guidance              Keyword Underline            │
├─────────────────────────────────────────────────────────────────┤
│ Position     : Executive   Manager   Engineer                     │
│ Purpose      : Plan (planning)  Do (countermeasure)  See (risk finding) │
│ Skill level  : Novice   Expert                                    │
├─────────────────────────────────────────────────────────────────┤
│ Do it ☐                                                           │
├─────────────────────────────────────────────────────────────────┤
│ Civil approval delay due to differences in loading data between civil and │
│ equipment subcontractors                                          │
│                                                                   │
│ From the point of view of establishing the company reputation     │
│                                                                   │
│ Your participants/elements concerned are:                         │
│  Company   Client   Government   Industry   Public opinion        │
│  Journalism   Foreign country                                     │
│ Click the one which is the source of your concern.                │
└─────────────────────────────────────────────────────────────────┘
```

Figure 7.13. Association guidance for executives.

the executive is to focus on "establishing the company reputation." The executive's participants are company, client, government, industry, public opinion, journalism, and foreign country.

7.3 EVALUATION AND OTHER POTENTIAL APPLICATIONS*

7.3.1 Positive Evaluation

Users (project managers) can use the knowledge base effectively by implementing the human–computer cooperative system in order to obtain associ-

---

*Most material in this section is adapted from Niwa, 1988b.

ation knowledge from the knowledge base in addition to knowledge by existing inference methods. For example, they could integrate different kinds of knowledge in a real-world context that could not have been anticipated when the knowledge base was implemented. This was especially effective for risk management of large construction projects. Similarly, the human–computer cooperative system will be applied to other ill-structured management domains and most real-world problems that require the integration of different specialists.

Project managers were considerably satisfied using the human–computer cooperative system. This is largely because the cooperative system enabled explicit user participation in the knowledge association subsystem; user participation is important for good advisory interactions. Moreover, the explicit user participation made it possible for the system to provide different answers for the different users. This overcame, to some extent, the users' complaints that the answers that existing expert systems had provided were too predictable.

The human–computer cooperative system enabled knowledge engineers to elicit considerable knowledge from the knowledge suppliers in the knowledge base implementation phase. This is because the human–computer cooperative system permitted nonrelated knowledge to be incorporated into the knowledge base; such knowledge is integrated by using the knowledge association subsystem in the knowledge utilization phase. If it did not permit nonrelated knowledge, the heavy burden on knowledge suppliers, in determining knowledge relationships in such a huge and ill-structured domain as project management, might result in their refusing to supply the knowledge requested.

Knowledge relationships (i.e., rules) were added in the knowledge base as a result of using the human–computer cooperative system. This implies that the system may also be regarded as a tool for knowledge acquisition, which is one of the most critical themes in knowledge engineering. The advantage of this tool is that acquired rules are rather vivid because knowledge relationships are determined when they are used in a real-world problem context (i.e., not in the knowledge base implementation phase, but in the knowledge base utilization phase).

It was easy to obtain consensus among the people concerned with the system development, because the human-computer cooperative system involved subsystems that used existing expert system techniques (i.e., forward and backward reasoning). Even if users refused to take advantage of the cooperative function, the system would still provide existing expert system level performance. Smooth development toward a new system is essential for users to accept it.

7.3.2   Negative Evaluation

Some engineers expressed concern when they learned that the system did not always provide the same answers, but that the answers were dependent on the user's responses. This concern may be natural for "rigid domains" (e.g., plant control and process control domains). In such domains, high system reliability means providing the same answers in the same situations; in other words, the answers should be independent of the differences in users. However, in the ill-structured management domains, it is proper for the system to give answers that depend on the user's responses, just as human consultants do with their human clients.

Some staff, who were often research scientists of management science, worried about a greater burden on users employing the cooperative system as opposed to those employing ordinary expert systems. This greater burden was due to explicit user participation in knowledge association subsystems. They thought that this was an obstacle to efficient problem solving. However, the point to be emphasized here should be problem-solving effectiveness and user satisfaction.

7.3.3   Future Research Items

Future research should investigate additional items, such as those listed below:

- Increase the sophistication of the procedure for converting point of view.
- Investigate and develop guide functions of human intuitive ability in addition to converting point of view.
- Develop an evaluating or learning mechanism of guide functions for human intuitive ability.
- Apply the cooperative system to other ill-structured domains (e.g., DSS) in order to identify its practical shortcomings for future improvement.
- Expand the system as an experimental tool for human and computer interface research. This will contribute to improving the system.

- Improve the system as a knowledge acquisition tool that effectively uses human intuitive ability.

7.3.4 Potential Applications to Other Fields

There may be many other potential fields for the successful development of human–computer cooperative systems. From the preceding discussions, we can determine the expected characteristics of such fields:

1. Specialists' knowledge, obtained through experience rather than scientific knowledge, will play a central role, and
2. There will be rather ill-structured fields, in which structure and function cannot be completely determined and therefore trial and error will have to be used for problem solving, or
3. There will be multispecialty fields, in which integrated use of knowledge is required for effective problem solving, even if knowledge among several specialties is not well related when the knowledge base is implemented.

Manufacturing fields, in their traditional sense, for example, do not seem to have these features because such fields largely consist of machines, assembly lines, or plants that are very rigidly structured and require scientific knowledge for their operation. However, for improving productivity of the manufacturing domains, some strategies have recently been proposed (Whitmore, 1987). Some of them include the following:

a. Problem control should be targeted at the manager's office rather than on the assembly line.
b. Line production, staff management, workers, and supervision should be more closely linked and integrated.
c. Management should involve teaching, communicating, and monitoring all workers.

Item a corresponds to items 1 and 2, b corresponds to items 1 and 3, and c corresponds to items 1, 2, and 3.

An enormous variety of business fields certainly have the above three features. However, most computerization efforts in such fields (e.g., office automation) have so far focused primarily on the very rigid aspects of such fields because of the ease in applying existing computer technologies. Recently, many expert systems have begun to appear in business fields (e.g., Silverman, 1987). This may be considered as a first step in applying our human–computer cooperative concept because people will begin to really notice the needs for human–computer cooperative systems after they use today's expert systems and discover their limitations in real-world, ill-structured problem solving.

7.4 SUMMARY

This chapter proposed a new concept—a "human-computer cooperative system"—based on the discussion about the future trends of the roles of computers. This system includes (1) a knowledge base, (2) a computer inference function, and (3) human intuitive ability. To achieve the cooperation of 2 and 3, (4) a guide function of human intuitive ability is incorporated into a computer. This concept was applied to knowledge association. When initial knowledge is given, the computer helps the user to recall keywords by providing appropriate suggestions. This corresponds to 4. With the help of the computer, the user recalls keywords by using his intuitive (association) ability. This corresponds to 3. When the keywords are entered by the user, the computer uses its retrieval/pattern-matching ability to search its knowledge base and provides association knowledge that includes the keywords. This corresponds to 1 and 2.

A human–computer cooperative system for project risk management was developed. The system consisted of forward reasoning, backward reasoning, and knowledge association. The former two subsystems utilized existing expert system techniques, and the third was our newly proposed subsystem that used human association ability. The users could make effective use of the knowledge base because the two reasoning subsystems provided logically related knowledge in the knowledge base, and because the last subsystem could extract nonlogically related knowledge from the knowledge base.

User evaluations of the system were described, which included the following five positive aspects:

1. Effective use of the knowledge base,
2. User satisfaction due to explicit participation,
3. Efficient knowledge elicitation from knowledge suppliers,

4. New knowledge (rule) acquisition methods during the knowledge utilization phase, and

5. Ease of obtaining consensus of system development

To apply human–computer cooperative systems to other fields, expected characteristics of these fields were identified: (1) domain specialists' knowledge will play a central role, and they will be (2) rather ill-structured or (3) multispecialty fields. There are many fields, especially management and business fields, that will effectively use human–computer cooperative systems.

REFERENCES

Niwa, K., "Knowledge-based human–computer cooperative system for ill-structured management domains," *IEEE Transactions on Systems, Man, and Cybernetics*, **SMC-16**(3), p. 335, 1986.

Niwa, K., "Human–computer cooperative system: Conceptual basis, sample system evaluation, and R&D directions," *Proc. of American Society of Mechanical Engineers Manufacturing International*, p. 87, 1988b.

Silverman, B. G. (ed.), *Expert Systems for Business*, Addison-Wesley, Reading, MA, 1987.

Whitmore, K. R., "Management for productivity," *MIT Report*, p. 3, September 1987.

SUGGESTIONS FOR DISCUSSION

1. Using Fig. 7.1, explain what is meant by "thinking support."

2. Why do you agree or disagree with the trend of the main roles of computers indicated in Fig. 7.1?

3. Can you think of other structures of human–computer cooperation in knowledge association (see Fig. 7.2)?

4. In the personified dialog between human and computer (from H1 to H11), discuss the differences between this dialog and

   • Ordinary expert system dialogs, and

   • Human–human consultant dialogs.

5. It has been suggested that in ill-structured management domains it is proper for systems to give answers that depend on user responses. Why do you agree or disagree?

6. Give example domains of engineering, management, or marketing fields that can use human–computer cooperative systems in addition to project risk management.

_____8
LESSONS FOR SUCCESSFUL IMPLEMENTATION

This chapter presents 19 lessons for successful implementation of knowledge-based systems. These lessons were obtained during the course of 10 years of research and implementation of knowledge-based systems (including ordinary expert systems and human–computer cooperative systems) for project risk management of large construction projects. These lessons are described in the three phases of system planning, system development, and system maintenance. These lessons are addressed directly to researchers and developers for developing knowledge-based systems. However, at the same time, these lessons will also be useful for system users and system clients because mutual understanding and cooperation with researchers/developers and users/clients is essential to successful implementation of knowledge-based systems.

8.1 SYSTEM PLANNING PHASE

System planning starts off with inquiries from clients, involves making system conceptual plans including system development strategies, and ends in obtaining authorized go-aheads for system development.

1. *Select problems that are directly relevant to end users.* Researchers and developers often receive inquiries about the possibility of developing

"pilot" knowledge-based systems from potential users. In our experience, middle management in various fields often asks us these questions because top management has asked them the same questions. Top management inquiries often occurred just after they had read newspaper articles indicating that their competitors were developing knowledge-based systems. This means that these inquiries are not always derived from "real" needs of their companies and therefore do not always proceed to actual development. Engineering people (e.g., those in EDP departments) also asked us these questions. They were very eager to create knowledge-based systems. There was excellent cooperation with them in developing pilot systems because they were interested in AI and knowledge engineering. They devoted their time entirely to implementing the system. However, this cooperation suddenly stopped when the pilot system was developed. They never wanted to deliver it to expected end users to demonstrate and sell it. The system was their "toy" (Niwa, 1988a). Both cases taught us that if we want to develop real systems that are used by end users, we have to distinguish real needs from among a number of inquiries.

2. *Avoid problems that can be solved by traditional methods.* If a problem can be solved by traditional methods such as operations research, information retrieval, or filing systems, researchers and developers should explain this to their clients because in such cases traditional methods are often better than AI technologies. Sometimes, upon hearing this, certain clients become disappointed because they want to be users of the "most advanced technology" (i.e., AI). A desirable policy with such clients is to tell them that "the problem can be solved primarily by traditional methods; however, this does not necessarily exclude AI. If AI is suitable for solving some of the problems, we will apply AI technologies in those areas." However, if the client still insists on AI, the order should be avoided because such clients only want to apply AI rather than solve problems.

3. *Avoid projects that may be strongly opposed by some of the participants concerned.* There are many individuals and organizations that are concerned with developing a knowledge-based system for a certain domain. In the beginning of the system planning phase, researchers and developers and even clients/users are apt to ignore those who seem to be against the project. However, this may often result in the system not being implemented. This lesson was obtained from our experience as briefly described below. A project management department of a certain large engineering company asked us to develop a project risk management system. A joint

study with the project management department indicated that a system that would calculate risk contingency would be useful as well as feasible. A pilot system was built and demonstrated to the participants. However, an actual system was never implemented because the proposal management department was very much concerned about situations in which the system would determine large contingencies.

4. *Involve actual end users from the beginning.* System development projects are sometimes initiated not by actual end users but by department heads or staff. In addition, funding of projects is often provided by department heads. In such cases, developers are likely to regard the end users as only interviewees in determining the system requirements. "If a technically good system can be implemented, then users will be pleased to use it. Therefore, it is only necessary for technical experts to work intensely in order to create a good system." This is often a principle of developers in the project planning phase. However, during this phase it is important to involve the actual end users so that they and the developers can cooperate in making the system plan. Such cooperation generally results in good plans and user satisfaction. Otherwise, users are sometimes reluctant to agree to a project plan, which may cause rejection or delay of the project. Although go or no-go decisions should be made by the department head who initiates and funds the project, users should be asked about the system.

5. *Establish strategies to obtain the collaboration of knowledge suppliers.* The most distinguished feature in developing knowledge-based systems (rather than other computer systems) is that they cannot be successfully developed and maintained without the collaboration of knowledge suppliers. Expected knowledge suppliers have not usually been included in system development project teams; rather, members generally consist of researchers, developers, and users/clients. Therefore, one of the effective strategies in obtaining the collaboration of knowledge suppliers is to include them in a project team from the system planning phase. However, knowledge suppliers are not usually interested in joining a project team because this brings no profit to them. Consequently, it is sometimes necessary to redefine the system scope and objectives so that the system will provide the knowledge suppliers with some profit. For example, our project risk management system users initially included a department head, staff, and senior prior managers. However, the scope of users was extended to junior project managers and major project personnel such as attorneys, accountants, manufacturing managers, transportation managers, installation supervisors, inspectors,

and so on. This was because their knowledge was essential for project risk management, and the way to effectively obtain their collaboration (including effectively collecting their knowledge) was to let them be system users and, at the same time, project team members (Niwa, 1988a).

6. *Obtain top management support for project take-off.* Top management support is important to project take-off. Project advantages are not necessarily recognized by all persons concerned. Therefore, obtaining top management support can affect people's attitudes, which will increase the possibility of project success. One of the effective strategies in obtaining top management support is to show them pilot system demonstrations.

8.2   SYSTEM DEVELOPMENT PHASE

System development involves organizing system development projects, designing and developing knowledge-based systems, as well as designing organizations or procedures for knowledge acquisition.

7. *Let users think that they have developed the system.* Users are sometimes reluctant to use systems that they have not created. This is well known as the NIH (not invented here) problem. Therefore, for successful application of systems it is important for users to think that *they* have developed such systems. Strategies taken in our project to achieve this are as follows. A project leader was appointed by the department head of major users. Under this project leader, two subleaders were appointed: one was a researcher/engineer and the other was a manager of users. The objective of this organization was to encourage users to take initiative in the project, although technical subleaders sometimes played substantial roles in the project.

8. *Study and understand domain knowledge and problems.* Since "power is knowledge" (Feigenbaum, 1977; Lenat and Feigenbaum, 1987) in knowledge-based systems, system developers must understand the meaning of each piece of knowledge that will be stored in knowledge bases. This is necessary because system developers have to develop systems that will not output extremely unreasonable answers. Generally, knowledge-based systems do not guarantee "right" answers, but rather depend on how knowledge pieces have been represented in knowledge bases. In addition,

system developers' understanding of domain knowledge and problems is also necessary for efficient system development. Without this it is very difficult for them to effectively communicate with users and extract knowledge from knowledge suppliers. A desirable level of understanding of domains by system developers is that achieved by consultants.

9. *Clarify what users really need.* Meeting all possible user requirements is an invariable principle; however, this does not necessarily mean that all such requirements should be accepted in their original form. It is well known that researchers and developers do not always understand user requirements. Sometimes *users* do not understand their own requirements. This double misunderstanding often occurs when new systems such as knowledge-based systems or human–computer cooperative systems are being developed because it is rather difficult for users to anticipate all possible situations. Developing and showing pilot functions of user requirements, and discussing user system functions from a wider viewpoint (e.g., in our project, desirable computer roles in information-intensive societies) are effective in dealing with this.

10. *Avoid insisting on existing AI techniques in determining system functions (inputs/outputs).* The purpose of developing a system in actual management fields is primarily to solve or assist in solving problems for users, not merely to apply existing AI techniques. (Of course, there may be exceptions such as AI feasibility studies or doctoral researches in AI.) Therefore, system functions (inputs/outputs) should be determined primarily based on user needs and not technical viewpoints. Otherwise, technically biased system functions may be created, which may result in system refusal by users.

11. *Foster mutual understanding between system developers and users.* To determine system functions, it is necessary for system developers and users to understand each other. This is, however, very difficult because they generally have different ways of thinking as well as different terminology. A strategy used to overcome this problem was to start discussions about easily understandable functions. Thus, functions related to information retrieval were first discussed, and users and developers became accustomed to each other's terminology. Then, functions related to knowledge inference were discussed. Since the meaning of "inference" is more strict than that in everyday conversation, it was necessary for system developers to explain it by easy examples as well as by showing how it differs from information retrieval. Finally, functions related to human–computer cooperation were

discussed because new system concepts are generally difficult to understand by users without background knowledge.

12. *Authorize knowledge suppliers to provide their knowledge.* It is rather difficult and time consuming for knowledge suppliers to provide knowledge obtained through their experience because this involves remembering suitable situations, identifying structures (e.g., causes) of situations (this becomes "knowledge"), evaluating knowledge in relation to system purposes, and representing it clearly to other people. Knowledge suppliers may be too busy to provide knowledge for *future* systems. Therefore, knowledge suppliers should at least be authorized to provide knowledge (Niwa, 1988a).

13. *Encourage knowledge suppliers to tell about negative experiences.* In project risk management systems, negative experience (i.e., risk) plays an important part in the knowledge base. Therefore, a number of such experiences were collected. Difficulties were met in collecting such knowledge, although lesson 5 (let knowledge suppliers be system users) and lesson 12 (authorize knowledge provision) were applied. Two more strategies were created to encourage knowledge suppliers to tell about *risks*. These involve interviewing established or top class project managers, who tend not to be adversely affected by the disclosure of negative stories, and who regard this as a responsibility of established project managers. The other strategy involves collecting near-miss experiences. There are a number of near-misses that occur with each risk that actually happened. Collecting such near-misses is as important as collecting actual risks. Knowledge suppliers were pleased to tell about these near-misses.

14. *Be cautious in establishing access to knowledge sources (knowledge suppliers or original documents).* There are many documents related to every piece of knowledge that was gathered from project managers. In our system, for every risk there are many related documents such as trouble reports, claim reports, drawings, photographs, progress reports and so on. Knowledge base users often require such related information. It is useful for users if related information can be easily retrieved or if knowledge suppliers can be easily identified by the users. However, caution is necessary in achieving this in order to ensure privacy. The method used here attached a related document number to every piece of knowledge, and to allow users to inquire about related documents and knowledge suppliers by contacting the system maintenance group.

8.3   SYSTEM MAINTENANCE PHASE

The main activities in the maintenance phase of knowledge-based systems are to maintain knowledge bases, to encourage system users in using systems, and to identify system defects for future improvement.

15. *Assign full-time personnel to system maintenance.* Very often part-time members are assigned to system development projects and system maintenance projects. They are usually representatives of related departments. Even if this personnel management is successful in system development projects, it is not necessarily applied to system maintenance project. System development is generally exciting, especially if the system is new; this is a major reason why members of system development projects are pleased to work even if they are not full-time members. On the other hand, system maintenance is not as exciting as system development because of major routine work. However, good system maintenance is one of the most crucial factors in system use. Therefore, it is necessary to assign full-time system maintenance personnel.

16. *Establish an "automatic" or "attractive" knowledge acquisition organization.* Maintaining knowledge bases is a key to successful utilization of knowledge-based systems. "Knowledge maintenance meetings" were organized, which were held once a month or once every two months. In addition, a three-day meeting at a resort hotel was held two times a year. The members of such meetings were senior project personnel (10–15 persons) of related departments as well as system maintenance project members. The major purpose of these meetings was to examine and correct/complement information on the questionnaires gathered from many project personnel so that it could be entered into the knowledge base. From the point of view of members of related departments, the other purposes were for them to be able to learn the new information in the questionnaires, and to be able to become acquainted with other personnel, which improved informal networks among project personnel.

17. *Publish a user group newsletter.* If a system is not famous or not widely used, encouraging users to continuously use the system is sometimes necessary. A user group newsletter is effective in accomplishing this. In this situation, it is recommended that the system maintenance group publish such newsletters. Through newsletters, users can be informed of successful cases of system applications, which will encourage them to use the system.

In addition, they can also learn different methods of using the system, and about other users with whom they can discuss the system. Sometimes asking users to write articles for such newsletters is effective in refreshing their interest in the system. It should also be pointed out that active newsletters help to keep top management support.

18. *Don't ignore "unreasonable" user requests.* One of the most important activities in the system maintenance phase is identifying defects of the system or user complaints that will be used in the system planning phase for the next system versions. In this feedback loop, unreasonable user requests may become a trigger for researchers and developers to invent entirely new concepts or methods. For example, the idea of the human–computer cooperative system was largely based on an "unreasonable" request: "why do expert systems not perform knowledge association, whereas people do?"

19. *Overdependence on top management sometimes results in a system being discontinued.* Top management support is very important in the system planning phase, especially for system take-off, as described in lesson 6. However, in the system maintenance phase, overdependence on top management is very risky because changes in top management sometimes mean system changes. New top management generally will not support a system if it is widely known as "the former top management's system." They would rather start another system development project.

8.4   SUMMARY

Nineteen lessons were presented for successful implementation of knowledge-based systems:

System Planning Phase

1. Select problems that are directly relevant to end users.
2. Avoid problems that can be solved by traditional methods.
3. Avoid projects that may be strongly opposed by some of the participants concerned.
4. Involve actual end users from the beginning.
5. Establish strategies to obtain the collaboration of knowledge suppliers.
6. Obtain top management support for project take-off.

System Development Phase

7. Let users think that they have developed the system.

8. Study and understand domain knowledge and problems.

9. Clarify what users really need.

10. Avoid insisting on existing AI techniques in determining system functions (inputs/outputs).

11. Foster mutual understanding between system developers and users.

12. Authorize knowledge suppliers to provide their knowledge.

13. Encourage knowledge suppliers to tell about negative experiences.

14. Be cautious in establishing access to knowledge sources (knowledge suppliers or original documents).

System Maintenance Phase

15. Assign full-time personnel to system maintenance.

16. Establish an "automatic" or "attractive" knowledge acquisition organization.

17. Publish a user group newsletter.

18. Don't ignore "unreasonable" user requests.

19. Overdependence on top management sometimes results in a system being discontinued.

More sophisticated analyses are left for future research, which certainly will contribute to establishing an "implementation research" or "implementation theory" (e.g., Doctor et al., 1979; Schultz, 1987) on artificial intelligence and knowledge-based systems.

REFERENCES

Doctor, R., R. L. Schultz, and D. P. Slevin (eds.), *The Implementation of Management Science*, In R. Machol (ed.), TIMS Studies in the Management Sciences 13, North-Holland, New York, 1979.

Feigenbaum, E. A., "The art of artificial intelligence. I. Themes and case studies of knowledge engineering," *Proceedings of IJCAI-77*, p. 1014, 1977.

Lenat, D. B., and E. A. Feigenbaum, "On the thresholds of knowledge," *Proceedings of IJCAI-87*, P. 1173, 1987.

Niwa, K., "Knowledge transfer: A key to successful application of knowledge-based systems," *The Knowledge Engineering Review* 2(2), p. 147, 1988a.

Schultz, R. L., Special Issue, "Implementation," *Interface*, 17(3), 1987.

SUGGESTIONS FOR DISCUSSION

1. How can you identify actual user needs among many inquiries?

2. It has been suggested that problems that can be solved by traditional methods, such as operations research, information retrieval, or filing systems, should be avoided by AI. Do you agree or disagree?

3. Why is user involvement in system development projects necessary?

4. Why is the collaboration of knowledge suppliers important to implement knowledge-based systems?

5. If you were in top management, which factors would you be interested in when being shown demonstration systems?

6. How many different strategies can you think of to enable users to think that *they* have developed systems?

7. List and discuss effective ways of knowledge acquisition in the system maintenance phase.

8. Explain why and how top management support may be doubled-edged.

9
CONCLUDING REMARKS

This chapter discusses three aspects: human–computer cooperative systems, project risk management, and future research.

9.1 HUMAN-COMPUTER COOPERATIVE SYSTEMS

This book presents a new concept—a human–computer cooperative system—proposed as the basis for the design of the next generation of knowledge-based systems for ill-structured domains. The key element is incorporation of human intuitive ability into a computer system to improve its flexibility and applicability. More specifically, the system includes (1) a knowledge base, (2) a computer inference function, and (3) human intuitive ability. To achieve the cooperation of (2) and (3), (4) a guide function of human intuitive ability is incorporated into the system.

This concept was created because the effective use of human intuitive ability is a key to successful management or decision making in ill-structured domains. Thus, we developed methods for utilizing human intuitive ability.

About 10 years ago, when AI needed new concepts to solve actual (not toy) problems, expert systems appeared with the idea of incorporating human knowledge into computers. This was an epoch in AI history, since the emergence of expert systems has succeeded in significantly expanding the application fields of computers. Today, we are advancing into a postindustrial society in which new methods are needed that can solve ill-structured management problems. We think the human–computer cooperative system, with its idea of incorporating human intuitive ability into computer systems, is one of the earliest concepts to meet this need.

9.2   PROJECT RISK MANAGEMENT

This book presents a human–computer cooperative system for risk management of large construction projects. The purpose of the system is to reduce the recurrence of similar risks in the execution stage of large construction projects.

The system was developed according to four requirements. The first requirement (i.e., collecting large amounts of experience) established procedures for acquiring knowledge based on the analysis of domain knowledge. For the second requirement (i.e., to be adaptable to many projects), a standard work package method was developed that can use risk knowledge with any size project work package. With respect to the third requirement (i.e., to analyze the cause and risk mechanism), common expert system techniques (forward and backward reasoning) were found effective for project managers in determining risks in advance. For the fourth requirement (i.e., improved abilities), a knowledge association method was developed that retrieves nonlogically related knowledge from the knowledge base.

These methods have been successfully systematized into a new system (i.e., a human–computer cooperative system).

9.3   FUTURE RESEARCH

The human–computer cooperative system can be considered as a goal of goal-oriented strategy for future directions of expert systems, as described in Section 3.3. Therefore, in identifying and achieving desirable functions in more depth for human–computer cooperative systems, we probably have to consider the difference between humans and computers, which directly relates to exploring what human intelligence is. In other words, this system may become an experimental tool for investigating human intelligence in addition to performing practical roles in actual management fields. Researching human intelligence by using this system is left for future research activities.

The most important item of future R&D for project risk management is to develop methods that can treat completely new risks. (This book deals with preventing recurrence of similar risks. A method that can extract non-related knowledge from a knowledge base was developed. Thus, knowledge can be utilized in contexts that could not have been predicted when the knowledge base was implemented.) Completely new risks seem too difficult to treat by using human–computer cooperative systems and current AI technologies. Thus, ambitious people who develop this area may achieve significant advances in AI and management science.

SUGGESTIONS FOR DISCUSSION

1. Discuss the essence of human–computer cooperative systems.

2. Explain why human–computer cooperative systems can handle project risk management better than current expert systems.

3. Do you agree that human–computer cooperative systems can meet the needs of postindustrial or information-intensive societies?

4. It has been suggested that human–computer cooperative systems may also become experimental tools for investigating human intelligence. Explain why and how this will be possible.

5. Why is it very difficult to treat completely new risks by human–computer cooperative systems and current AI technologies?

INDEX